D1280297

JACQUES LOEW

FACE TO FACE WITH GOD

The Bible's Way to Prayer

translated by Alan Neame

PAULIST PRESS
New York/Ramsey, N.J./Toronto

First Published in Great Britain
by Darton, Longman and Todd Ltd
85 Gloucester Road, London SW7 4SU

©1977 Darton, Longman and Todd

Originally Published as *La Prière a L'Ecole des Grands Priants*
by Librairie Artheme Fayard, Paris.

Library of Congress
Catalog Card Number: 77-88179

ISBN: 0-8091-0227-7

Published by Paulist Press
Editorial Office: 1865 Broadway, New York, N.Y. 10023
Business Office: 545 Island Road, Ramsey, N.J. 07446

Printed and bound in the
United States of America

CONTENTS

[handwritten annotation beside "Praying with Mary": late 60s-70s 1977 was a dark period of Marian Piety resurge esp. after Medjugorje of '85 156k]

AUTHOR'S NOTE

The contents of this book originated in a series of weekly talks delivered at the *Ecole de la Foi* in Fribourg, Switzerland.

Not being a Biblical scholar or theologian myself, and with no other wish than to seek God and, with Philip, to say, 'I have found the man announced in the Law of Moses and the Prophets! He is Jesus son of Joseph, of Nazareth,' and further, with the Samaritan woman to declare, 'This must be the Christ!' I have been obliged to depend on many more learned authors for my source material. To all of these, whether named or unnamed in the text, I should like to express sincere thanks.

J. L.

INTRODUCTION

'Master, teach us to pray,' one of Jesus's disciples asked him. The disciple's name was never put on record. His request, nonetheless, unleashed the most unparalleled wave of prayer ever known in the history of the world: the Lord's Prayer repeated day after day, century after century, murmured millions of times over in the depths of the heart, chanted millions of times over by Christians keeping holiday.

It is appropriate that this disciple should have remained nameless and faceless. In his anonymity, like the Unknown Soldier, he represents us all. The unknown questioner personifies the anonymous multitude of which we, aware of our own ignorance of how to pray, form part. He stands for us: 'Master, teach us to pray.'

Be it said at the outset however, that prayer is not, in the first instance, a matter of speaking or of keeping silent, of pleading or of meditating, of time-honoured psalm or of spontaneous inspiration, but of coming face to face with God. Jesus revealed this to the Samaritan woman whom he met at Jacob's Well. When Jesus told the woman, 'If you only knew what God is offering and who it is now saying to you, "Give me a drink," you would have been the one to ask, and he would have given you the water of life,' (*Jn* 4:10), the Lord was giving us the essential key to prayer.

The first initiative comes from God: he is the one who first asks for a drink – who is thirsty for us. By beginning with this first 'Give me a drink,' Jesus is emphasising the essential order in prayer: God makes the first move, is always the first to speak. Our spiritual life, our life with God, is not, as it were, a game of patience which 'comes out' with luck if we play our cards right. It is a two-handed game, in which God always leads.

Hence, only when we have become aware of God's love, of God's begging for our love so that he can give us even more of his love – 'If you only knew what God is offering' – can we pray. Praying comes naturally, once we have sensed what God's gift is. 'If you only knew what God is offering and who it is now saying to you, "Give me a drink", you would have been the one to ask.' Prayer begins once we have realised that God wants to give us something very big.

Then, prayer re-attunes you, puts you in a sense on God's level, which is always higher than the one you would normally aim for. Prayer leads you to the source of living, as opposed to polluted, stagnant, waters. You reach the spring welling up from the 'deep' well – which is what you were looking for. 'You would have been the one to ask, and he would have given you the water of life.'

In learning how to pray, we are neither alone nor without guides: besides the unknown disciple and the Samaritan woman, there is that immense prayer-school, open for thousands of years. And studying the prayer-masters of the Old Testament, Jesus and his immediate disciples, and the saints of all the ages since, we shall discover the basic fact of all prayer: the Holy Spirit praying in us, the same Spirit which was the Primordial Breath sweeping over the waters before the creation of the world, the same Power of the Most High which took Mary under his protective shade.

But God, who created the universe and who one day 'will pitch his tabernacle among us,' would have us know by the same token that our prayer must be rooted in the circumstances of time and place at each stage and period of our lives. Unless our prayer is to be an artificial flower, it can only germinate, bloom and bear its fruit within the context of our everyday existence. And then on condition – we come back to the Samaritan woman – that our prayer is illuminated from above, by the light of the Word, whose aim is to 'enlighten everyone who comes into the world'.

By the same token too, we must not consider any event or person – be he Abraham, or Moses, or even Jesus – as being alone and unrelated, but as inescapably a part of God's universal design.

Now, this design – 'the Mystery' as St. Paul calls it – is not a hidden one. It is set out in the Bible and it is being worked out in the history of the Church.

In ancient Israel and the story of Moses, we see a people fleeing from slavery, marching towards a promised land – undertaking a march involving fatigue, rebellion, despair, yet spurred on by an even stronger hope. Scarcely however is the marvellous country attained when this same people is trapped in the snares of idolatry, and becomes corrupt. The destruction of Jerusalem and deportation to Babylon are the inevitable results. Then, in contact with the totalitarian sway of false gods, a little exiled remant rediscovers the unique grandeur of its mission: for it knows the true God, and the true God has chosen it as the instrument by which to make himself known to mankind. When this handful of people eventually comes back from exile, its only wish is to serve and worship this incomparable God. But, in no time at all, goodwill has once again ossified into customs and laws from which the letter has driven out the spirit.

Now, in the course of these events occupying something like two thousand years, another history is unfolding within the first. The promises, the covenants marking the lives of Abraham, Moses, Joshua, David, Solomon and Josiah; the prophecies of Isaiah, Amos, Jeremiah, Ezekiel and Hosea about what seem to be merely human events; in a word, this whole history of a nation on the march is revealed as being the preparation for a man who will prove to be the fulfilment of all those hundreds of years of tears and hopes – a messenger from God, a second Moses a hundred times more astonishing and marvellous, but also the son of David endowed with a divine unction of power, of wisdom, of consecration. And look – on a river-bank 'early in the morning', a morning as ordinary as any other, someone called Andrew goes over to his brother: 'We have found the Messiah, that is to say, the Christ!' He takes his brother to the man, who is about thirty and whom he has only known for two days, though his people have been waiting for him for two thousand years. His name is Jesus.

Less than three years go by, and the marvellous two-thousand-year dream falls to pieces. Jesus is crucified and dies, the victim of judicial murder. Andrew's brother, Simon-Peter, has meanwhile denied the Christ, though he has been his righthand man since the day when he said, 'You are the Christ, the son of the Living God.' There is nothing left for the few remaining supporters to do but bury the man who, they had believed, was to have been the one 'to set Israel free' (*Lk* 24:21).

And now, nearly two thousand years later, like Peter and others who gave their lives to make up for that one night's defection, we – that is to say, the new Israel – Italians, Swiss, Belgians, Mexicans, Japanese, Indians, Africans, Englishmen, peoples of all countries, all races, all nations, all languages and all cultures in every longitude and latitude – the fruit of the hope and expectation recorded on almost every page of the Bible – affirm that this same Jesus Christ is indeed he who has accomplished everything that was written in the Scriptures, 'in the Law of Moses, in the Prophets and in the Psalms,' (*Lk* 24:44). Like that first great convert, Paul of Tarsus, we say of this Christ that not only is he 'alive' (*Ac* 25:19) but that in him the very world is regenerated.

ABRAHAM

Entering the mystery of God

Some rivers have their sources in a damp patch in a field; others arise full-fledged, in abundant fountains beneath which an underground obstacle produces terrific pressure. So it is in the Old Testament: most of the time, awareness of the mystery of God is gradual, if not hesitant. Suddenly, then, through some individual or event, an inexhaustible density, an inexhaustible mass of faith is revealed. Thus, in the meanderings of *Genesis,* Abraham, our father in faith, emerges with incomparable force. Hundreds and thousands of years of stammering quest are concentrated and burst forth in him.

Nothing very remarkable on the face of it! 'Abram crossed the country to the holy place of Shechem, to the Oak of Moreh . . . Yahweh appeared to Abram and said, "I shall give this country to your posterity." And there Abram built an altar to Yahweh, who had appeared to him. Then he moved on eastwards of Bethel, pitching tent between Bethel and Ai. There he built an altar to Yahweh and invoked his name' (*Gn* 12:6–9).

So Abraham built altars: this surely doesn't mean that we should go about building oratories? What does it mean, then? As Abraham goes his nomadic way, he meets God; in the ordinary course of his peregrinations as he moves from place to place, he meets God. We also read, 'Abram went back to the place, where he had erected the previous altar, and there he invoked the name of Yahweh' (*Gn* 13:4). For Abraham, the whole world was a cathedral (an oak tree, some scattered stones); the whole world was God's temple for him.

This pre-supposes that we are in a state of prayer. Not a matter of many acts of prayer, but of a state of prayer in which we can meet God anywhere. If prayer is encountering the presence of God, we have to be attentive, on the alert. In a state of obedient friendship too, since the nomad's road is a road taken at God's command: 'Abram, leave your homeland!' Only after the act of obedience will Abraham meet God in the Promised Land.

His basic form of prayer therefore, through the long days and marches, will be this silent, attentive clinging to God, so well expressed by Jesus when he said, 'My Father never leaves me alone,' that is, the encounter is continuous, 'because I continuously do what pleases him' (*Jn* 8:29).

We all know that when we have experienced some great sorrow, bereavement or betrayal, whatever we do as we come and go, everything happening in the course of the day, is pervaded by this presence, by grief at this absence. It is the same with a great joy: nothing is too difficult to do, we can do anything we set our hands to. In the kitchen, the pots and pans rejoice at our joy. Thus it is, whether we are in a state of sadness or grief, or in a state of joy. And similarly, with Abraham who meets God everywhere, in anticipation of what St. Teresa of Avila said so pithily that you cannot better it: 'A friendly meeting with God, who you know loves you.' Abraham's heart is ready, since he has already listened to God and obeyed. Quite the opposite of Adam, who for his part hid to avoid meeting his Maker; Abraham is in a state of wishing for the friendly meeting.

'And there he invoked his name.' Abraham's prayer consists entirely in this invoking. No words. Not a subjective prayer, asking, pleading or even tongue-tied before so great a God. Faithful in advance to Jesus, Abraham does not multiply words (*Mt* 9:7) or imagery. He invokes the Name Most High, he acknowledges God as God, he stands in his presence; he adores, but does not conceptualise: 'You are none other than God.'

For Abraham, however, this God is still unknown: El Shaddai, 'God the Mountain-dweller', he who resides among the high peaks. After Moses, the name of God will be infinitely richer, but what does that matter! The important thing when invoking the name of God is to reach him in his own most personal aspect. Even if we know nothing about this great God, the very fact of saying 'My God', of saying 'Jesus', of saying 'Holy Spirit, come,' brings us into total intimacy with God, not felt maybe, but real. And we in any case can invoke our God, not only as the God of the inaccessible mountains in Abraham's way, but in St. Paul's way as 'the Father of our Lord Jesus Christ'. He whom Jesus has taught us to call 'Father': 'Father, glorify your name', that name indeed for the glory of which Jesus was to die.

To invoke the name of God is hence to affirm the ever-present intervention of God's love: 'I have made your name known to men' (*Jn* 17:6), that name being love: 'God loved the world so much that he gave his only Son' (*Jn* 3:16). 'O Father of our Lord Jesus Christ, who outdoing Abraham and Isaac have not spared your own Son for our sake, how could you not with him grant us every favour?' (Cf. *Rm* 8:32).

The saints tell us that, when we are tempted, we have only to invoke the name of Jesus: it will not make the temptation disappear, but it will give us the strength of his Spirit, since 'no one can say "Jesus is Lord" unless he is under the influence of the Holy Spirit' (1 *Co* 12:3). At this elevation, praying becomes part and parcel of apostolic preaching, that is to say, of bringing the name of Jesus to men.

Abraham did however have the advantage over us in one respect: he wasn't going too fast, not chasing Concorde to jump aboard before they shut the doors. He moved along at the same pace as his sheep, his camels and his wives. We too must not be going fast if we want to meet God. When you only have three minutes in which to catch the train and you look like missing it and the lights are against you, even if you say 'Jesus', or 'My Sweet' as Canadian nuns do, or if like many Englishmen you say 'B . . . . . ', there isn't all that much in it one way or the other. To invoke the name of Jesus, Son of the Living God, to be in a 'state of prayer', you have to go at God's pace and rid your life of complications.

As we look at Abraham, we make a second discovery: after the Promise, the meeting with God becomes a dialogue – a dialogue based on the Promise: 'Some time later,' that is, after

Abraham's defeat of the Four Kings, 'Yahweh's word came to Abraham in a vision: "Do not be afraid, Abram, I am your shield; your reward will be great." Abram replied, "My Lord Yahweh, what can you give me that is worthwhile, all the while I am childless?" Then, Yahweh's word came back to him in reply: "Look up at the sky and count the stars if you can . . . Such will be your posterity." Abram put his faith in Yahweh, who accounted this to his merit' (*Gn* 15:1–6).

Here again God takes the initiative. Every time we are going to pray, we are setting out to meet a God who is already waiting for us. 'Yahweh's word came to Abram.' God speaks first. Our words are only a response to a word, to the waiting, of God. And God's word, from Abraham to Mary and throughout history, is and always will be a word of peace: 'Do not be afraid' (*Lk* 1:30). How sweet this sounds to us in our lives today! Do not be afraid, leave your worries behind, even your intellectual ones. 'Do not be afraid, Abram, I am your shield, your reward.' Do not take this last word in its literal sense, but to mean 'I have something immense in store for you.'

When Abraham replies, he states simply and directly the fix that he is in. It is a real conversation, between the man and his God. 'My Lord Yahweh, what can you give me that is worthwhile, all the while I am childless?' That is his whole problem. Similarly, at the Annunciation, Mary will ask – and the dialogue is similar because the hearts of both are not rebellious, but receptive to the Word – 'How can this come about?' (*Lk* 1:34). They are not expressing doubt, not arguing the Divine Word; they are stating their problem. Whereupon, God confirms the Promise: 'Your heir will come from your own body' (*Gn* 15:5). 'Is it possible, Lord? You can see how I am!' and God confirms: 'Look up at the sky and count the stars if you can . . . Such will be your posterity.' Abraham has faith, and has faith in a promise which is humanly speaking impossible. St. Paul has a magnificent comment on this situation: 'Hoping against all hope', and this is the state which we enter by faith. 'He believed, and became the father of a multitude. He believed, and even the thought that his body was past fatherhood – he was about a hundred years old

– and that Sarah was too old to become a mother, did not shake his faith. Since God had made him a promise, incredulity did not make him hesitate' (*Rm* 4:18–20).

Are we convinced that this dialogue springs from God's promise, rather than from Abraham's own difficulties? But, this is already his act of hope: I believe, because you have promised this. 'Incredulity did not make him hesitate but, drawing strength from his faith and convinced that God had the power to do as he had promised, he gave glory to God' (*Rm* 4:20). This is the prayer of total conviction, of firm certainty in God. Anticipating any cry or plea, it is the conviction that God will accomplish what he has promised, since God takes pride in doing this. The Psalms and Prophets will tirelessly repeat this: 'Do not let us fall, the pagans will make fun of us, save us for the honour of your Name!'

Thus, like Abraham, to enter prayer, we must enter the promise. I pray, supported by God's promises: 'Incredulity did not make him hesitate.' Just so; to the man who asked Jesus to cure his epileptic son, 'If you can do anything, come and help us, take pity on us!' – 'If you can!' Jesus retorted, 'Everything is possible to someone who believes.' Immediately, the father of the child exclaims, 'I do believe! Supplement my little faith!' Jesus had in a sense reversed the man's prayer: 'If you can.' It is not whether Jesus can or cannot; it's the believer's faith that can do anything. Jesus is of course aware that his Father always helps him. And this is our permanent preparation for prayer: to rely on God alone and on God's promise to us. Prayer means going to meet God's promises.

The same situation arises a little further on (*Gn* 15:8): 'I am Yahweh who brought you out of Ur of the Chaldaeans to give you this country for you to own.' Abram replied, 'How am I to know that I shall own it?' – Tell me, give me a sign! – Fully confident, versed in Scripture, Mary doesn't even ask for a sign; all the same, God gives her one: 'Know this too, your kinswoman Elizabeth, though sterile, has conceived' (*Lk* 1:36).

Abraham believed Yahweh, and Yahweh accounted this as righteousness. This somewhat abstract word 'righteousness' is very simple to understand: Abraham 'put himself right' as regards God, he adjusted himself to God, as a qualified mechanic accurately adjusts one part of a machine to another. And hence, as Elizabeth said to Mary, so we can say to Abraham: 'Blessed are they who believe that the promise made to them by the Lord will come true.' Jesus himself was to say, 'Your ancestor Abraham rejoiced to think that he would see my day; he saw it and was glad' (*Jn* 8:56). Once again then, praying is not going into a church, but into a promise and relying on it.

The third discovery about prayer, still in *Genesis* 15, is contained in a mysterious sentence variously translated in different versions of the Bible, of which this is a fair rendering: 'When the sun was on the point of setting, a torpor fell on Abram, and a deep, dark dread descended on him' (*Gn* 15:12). In every religion, contact with God, with the sacred, with the mystery, perturbs and excites the fear of man. The sun is about to disappear. A torpor – this is mysterious, some translate it as 'trance' – falls on Abraham: 'Then a deep, dark dread descends on him.'

There are, it seems, two reasons for this darkness: on the one hand, the divine presence; and on the other, the task to be performed. The first is the unbearable weight of the Godhead, reducing frail human nature to helplessness. What the Bible calls the glory of God – his redoubtable presence and majesty – is a word derived from the root 'weight'. It is good to feel the distance between man and God. The man who has made some progress along the road, arrives like Abraham at a difficult moment: a deep, dark dread falls on him, a torpor.

We must not be surprised if, entering prayer, we enter darkness; this is because we are entering faith.

This is exactly what St. John of the Cross is telling us in his poem *One Dark Night*, when the soul sings of the happy adventure which she has experienced in going through the dark night of faith, and in emerging from that dark night to achieve union with her Beloved:

One dark night, when care flamed into love –

O wonderful adventure! – I slipped out unobserved,
in the wonderful darkness, secretly,
my household being asleep,
when no one could see me, nor I see anything,
with no light to guide me but what glowed in my heart . . .

'Secretly, in the wonderful darkness' – this exactly describes
entering the prayer of faith. The darkness described by St.
John of the Cross doesn't only fall on people like him. A
Brazilian friend of mine, called Gisah, a member of the first
intake at the *Ecole de la Foi* in Fribourg, made the same discovery. This was how she put it:
'Starting at the school wasn't easy. Towards the end of my
time there, I met people, but to begin with I had the feeling
that people were actually disappearing. When I got there, I
was more or less sure of myself, but then I developed a sense of
insecurity. I thought that I could help by putting myself at the
service of other people. I thought I already had some friends
and might make new ones. Ultimately, I felt quite alone. I
found no satisfaction and felt permanently alone; a desert had
come into existence all round me.'
Desert and darkness are the same thing.
'I then turned my attention to Him who was always there.
God began to take a different dimension. I used to read the Bible like a history-book relating to the past. Now, however,
everything began to come alive. Abraham comes to tell me of a
God who assures me: "I am your shield". Abraham certainly
goes into the darkness; nonetheless he still relies on God's
promise: "I am your shield". Jacob, for his part, shows me
that this God is faithful, even when we impose conditions on
him: "I am with you. I shall be with you".'
And everything comes alive. Let's see what she says next,
reminding ourselves that she is a Brazilian and that a
snowscape is a marvellous sight for her:
'I can explain this by a thought I had during a journey at
night.
'It was in winter. Sitting in the well-lit railway carriage, I
looked out of the window and, because of the lighting inside,
could see nothing of what was outside. I could only see myself

and the other people reflected back at me in the glass. At a
given moment, the carriage lights went out. Then everything
lit up outside: the snow, the darkness. I needed to be in the
dark myself, surrounded by darkness, before I discovered this
wonderful sight. I then applied this to the Bible. Divine
teaching methods have not changed: the desert is always the
place where we meet God.'

'A dark dread fell on him.' Though we have to suffer like
Abraham in the darkness, simply relying on the Promise, we
can be sure that meeting God cannot occur in any other way.
Long before the days of St. John of the Cross, St. John the
Evangelist was saying of Jesus: 'He is the light that enlightens
everyone' (*Jn* 1:9). And this tells us that the darkness does exist.

And now the second reason for the darkness, for the terror
falling on us. – Abraham had prepared a sacrifice, which God
had commanded him to offer: 'Lord Yahweh, how am I to
know that I shall really own this country?' ... Yahweh
replied, 'Fetch me a she-goat.' Abraham produced animals,
cut them in half lengthways, laid the halves opposite each
other according to the ancient covenantal procedure observed
between human-beings; birds of prey swooped down on the
carcases and Abraham chased them away (*Gn* 15:8–11). Thus
Abraham prepares the sacrifice demanded by God, and then
finds himself for the rest of the day having to fend off birds of
prey, regarded as ill-omened in his times. This demonstrates
the second worry that besets the apostle.

The first terror is that which seizes the contemplative at the
majesty of God. But this second one is apostolic: you have
worked all day carrying out God's orders, and on top of all
that you have to battle with birds of prey, with everything
militating against and preventing the sacrifice (which is the
will of God) from being performed. Abraham can do no more,
he goes into a state of fear and torpor. The three Apostles in
Gethsemane, similarly, were to fall asleep with sorrow at the
very moment of the Lord's supreme prayer.

The message which Abraham eventually receives from God
solves nothing: 'You should know that your descendants will
be exiles in a country not their own, to be enslaved an   op-

pressed for four hundred years. But eventually they will leave and I shall pass judgment on that nation . . . As regards yourself . . .' The message is at once cruel ('Your descendants as yet unborn will be strangers, slaves, oppressed for four centuries') and, for Abraham himself, consoling: 'You will join your ancestors in peace, you will be buried at a happy old age' (*Gn* 15:13–14).

So torpor and darkness do not exclude peace. The dark night of the contemplatives – Carthusians and Trappists say so and live so – exceeds anything that we can imagine. These great contemplatives may play no part in contemporary events, they do not watch each successive disaster, famine and war on television, yet they penetrate far further into the depths of man, into the depths of his potentialities for disaster and achievement. They are at the very source of all the images of disaster we see on television, having penetrated to the essence of the tragedy of human existence.

The apostle may well be beset with gloom, gloom which is compounded of mankind's running sores: slavery, abortion, galloping over-population, the insoluble problems with which we live.

To pray is to accept the night of faith, of obstacles, of suffering. We must beware of trying to get things done in too much of a hurry. As St. John of the Cross says, 'Many people make no progress; setting out along the path of virtue, and our Lord wanting to put them into the dark night, so that they can pass from this into union with God, they never come out the other side, since the darkness brings them to a halt.'

Finally, we have Abraham's last great stance as regards prayer; his intercession for Sodom (*Gn* 18:17–32). Here again, God takes the initiative. He asks the question, 'Shall I hide what I am about to do from Abraham?' God confronts Abraham with the situation, intending to rouse him to intercede. That is why God says, 'The crime of Sodom and Gomorrah is great; their sin is very grave!'

There are many things to be noted here. First of all, Abraham's simultaneous humility and boldness of heart. This is what fits him to undertake intercessory prayer. Abraham says, 'It is very bold of me to speak to the Lord, I who am but dust and ashes.' A humble man, he knows 'of what dust we are made', as the psalm says; but knowing that we are dust allows him to address God in all boldness.

Compare Abraham's attitude in the sacred bargaining which he is about to conduct with God, and his attitude to Lot and the neighbouring kings. In the latter case, it was a purely personal matter between Abraham and his nephew, or between Abraham and the kings: 'For me, nothing.' He asks for nothing! But in the case of Sodom, a whole people is concerned. Others are concerned. In this case, God wants Abraham to intercede for the people.

In Lot's case, Abraham did not make up a prayer – of the so-called 'universal' type – in which he might have said, 'O God, enlighten poor Lot! I think this . . . I think that.' You know, one of those ingenious prayers in which we dismantle someone else's character under the pretext of conversing with God! He proceeds very directly, letting Lot have the first choice. Abraham doesn't say anything to Lot, since the whole matter is Lot's business, not his. In the case of Sodom, on the other hand, an entire people is involved. Hence the bargaining for mercy begins; and this is Abraham's intercession. How fine it is –

'You must not think of doing such a thing! Won't you spare the city for the sake of fifty innocents inside it?' – 'You must not think of doing such a thing! to make the innocent perish with the guilty, so that innocent and guilty fare alike.' – 'You must not think of doing such a thing! Is the Judge of the whole earth not to act justly?'

Once again Abraham relies on God's promise. He doesn't rely on himself, even less on the merits of the people concerned. No. But the result turns out to be that the righteous can obtain forgiveness for the guilty; and this is the marvellous message which emerges from the text; this bargaining for mercy is acceptable to God.

'It's very bold of me to speak to the Lord, I who am but dust and ashes, but what if the fifty innocent should be five short? Would you destroy the whole city for these five?'

'Not if I find forty-five!'

'What if there are only forty?'

'I won't do it for the sake of the forty!'

'I trust the Lord will not be impatient if I go on. What if there are only thirty there?'

'I won't do it if I only find thirty there!'

'Again I make bold to address the Lord; what if there are only twenty?'

'I shan't wreak havoc for the sake of the twenty!'

'I trust the Lord won't be angry if I speak this last time. What if there are only ten?'

'I shan't bring destruction for the sake of the ten!'

Abraham didn't dare go any further! He might have done. He didn't dare to go down to one. Jeremiah was later to remark, 'One righteous man would have been enough!' 'Rove through the streets of Jerusalem, look and observe, search her markets and see if you can find a man, one man who does right, who strives for truth; so that I can pardon her, says Yahweh' (*Jr* 5:1).

Abraham stopped halfway. He could have gone down to one. Ezekiel has much to say in the same strain: the people have piled rapine on rapine, violence on violence, oppressing the poor, ill-treating strangers. Then Yahweh speaks: 'I have been looking for one of them to build the wall and man the breach against me, to defend the country and prevent me from destroying it; but I have found no one' (*Ez* 22:30).

Thus, the intercessor fights, 'manning the breach' and groaning because he can see that 'no one invokes your Name, no one bestirs himself to hold fast to you' (*Is* 64:16).

Can Abraham be blamed for having stopped at *ten*? Hardly! Even if he had gone down to *one*, he wouldn't have found anyone, since all this, in the last analysis, was in preparation for the unique intercessor: Jesus. But we, for our part, can be sure, in our huge, cruel, anonymous cities, every time that we go into a church, that the Righteous Man, the Life-Saver, is there, present in the Eucharist.

In conclusion be it said: intercessory prayer doesn't make the wild and absurd claim of influencing God or of making him change his mind. But it does enter into God's orbit, it enters the divine zone of attraction, where interaction takes place between ourselves and God. Everything comes from God, from his free decision that my prayer should be the cause of an effect. God tells Abraham what is happening, so that Abraham can begin to intercede. And the fulfilment of what God wishes or promises depends to some extent on my fidelity. Even a gigantic planet is influenced by the little moon circling round it.

Such then is praying as taught by Abraham; meeting God everywhere, a God beyond all frontiers, invoking the Name of God, entering the Promise, accepting the night of faith and the darkness, and then interceding for others.

JACOB

Wrestling with God

Let us now think about Jacob's strife, the strife of prayer, and more particularly about three characteristics common to all prayer and to all struggle: patience, perseverance and constancy, so long as the ordeal lasts. Three harsh facts, but all three nonetheless the paths of hope, which for its part 'is not deceptive' (*Rm* 5:5). All the same, I am not quite sure how to begin. As in any Christian mystery – death and resurrection for instance – there is a grim aspect to the struggle, and a glorious one. If I start by discussing perseverance and constancy, I begin with the grim aspect. If I start with Jacob, we shall see the results of the struggle before we have begun. Since the reader however, may, if so inclined, skip a few pages and go on to the more agreeable part of the chapter, we may as well begin with the austere aspect of the subject. Hope, then, even though still distant, is the reason for these words and the other two related concepts: endurance, steadfastness of heart. St. James tells us that a disciple must live by these truths until the Lord's return (5:7). Patience, perseverance and constancy lead to hope, and in the Bible hope is always linked with prayer. Hope: prayer.

The Strife of Prayer

Let us look at the words a little more closely. Patience comes from the Latin word *pati*, which means to suffer, to bear. Patience is not merely waiting, but suffering, bearing; and *patientia, impatientia* (patience, impatience) mean the ability or inability to bear. If we are able to bear, we are patient. If unable, then impatient.

The word perseverance contains the word 'severe' (*severus*), which originally used to mean inflexible, austere. To persevere means to continue, to persist, to be inflexible. As for constancy, this denotes the quality of standing up (*stare*), of someone holding himself up straight, of having poise. And this in turn leads on to notions of stability, of permanence. A constant, derived from the same root, is something that does not vary. Hence the word constant means firm; and constancy means firmness. The same root *stare* has also given rise to the words 'stature' and 'statue' – a person standing upright. And *stare* is also at the root of that learned word, of key importance to the philosophers of old: substance. Substance, far from being indeterminate or vague, is that which is permanent in a being or thing otherwise subject to change, and which hence maintains its identity.

As for the word endurance, this comes from an ancient word *duramen*, which used to be applied to the old wood of the vine, the stock so contorted and knotted as to be uncuttable. Hence, the words 'endurance' meaning ability to bear; and 'duration' meaning length of time. All these words, patience, perseverance, constancy, endurance, very frequently recurring in the Gospel, contain, as you see, the notion of strength and duration.

What does Scripture tell us about this? – for that alone can show us the realities behind the words. As ever, when we open the Bible and 'search the Scriptures', we have to use a bi-focal approach. First, we plunge our eyes into the Mystery of God: to search for the meaning of these words. And then, from contemplating our self-revealing God, we pass on to considering what someone's attitude should be who is trying to model himself on God. As far as we Christians are concerned, constancy and perseverance are not virtues to be discovered in the pages of some sage, philosopher or scholar, but to be sought in God himself. We look at God: what has he told us about himself? And, starting from him, what can we discover for ourselves to practice? And as we look at God, we should do well to look at him in three aspects: as 'the God of our forefathers, Abraham, Isaac and Jacob', as the God of the prophets and inspired writers of the Old Testament, and as the Word made flesh, Jesus Christ.

So we have three stages: the mystery of God revealed in Jesus Christ, and finally our own attitude as taught us by God through his own example in the Lord Jesus. Forthwith, these qualities drawn from the Bible take on an altogether grander dimension than mere human virtues or ascetical exercises. They form a loving imitation of our God.

In the Old Covenant, we see how Israel gradually became aware, over the years and centuries, that its long history from the Flood and the saving of Noah was 'the time of divine patience', 'The time of divine patience' (*Rm* 3:26) was St. Paul's expression for the lengthy duration of Old Testament times, the period in which, anticipating the Cross of Jesus and justification by faith in Jesus, God mercifully restrained his anger and allowed sins to go unpunished. Seeing our wretchedness, God waits; he does not repay on the nail. And thus God reveals his tenderness. 'Yahweh, Yahweh, God of tenderness and compassion, slow to anger, rich in kindness and fidelity, maintaining his kindness to thousands and tolerating fault, transgression and sin' (*Ex* 34:6–7).

Such was the era of the Old Testament, of divine patience, and of every period during it, as the psalmists were aware: 'Yahweh is tenderness and pity, slow to anger, full of love, his resentment does not last forever, his indignation does not last for long' (*Ps* 103:8–9). Isaiah noted the same divine fact: 'For the sake of my Name, I deferred my anger; for the sake of my Honour, I curbed it' (*Is* 48:9). And Jeremiah, confronted by his persecutors, even complained that God was a little too patient: 'Your anger is too slow, do not let me be abducted by these people' (*Jr* 15:15). The whole purpose of this patience was Jesus, 'who was appointed by God to sacrifice his life to win reconciliation through faith' (*Rm* 3:25); but the divine patience was already active, as St. Peter was to observe, 'while God was patiently waiting for Noah to build the ark, in which a small number were saved by means of water, which prefigures baptism which saves you now' (1 *P* 3:20). Yes, God temporises because of his longanimity, and this consists in wanting to save, not half a dozen people from the Flood, but all mankind from sin.

Patience is not weakness; be sure of that. We shall discover in the *Book of Jonah* that God's patience extends to the heathen until they have been converted. This then is what we have to admire, what must inspire us – the tireless patience of God as he waits. 'I take no pleasure in the death of anyone – oracle of Lord Yahweh. Repent and live!' (*Ez* 18:32).

Jesus himself may be called 'God's patience', God's patience made visible. Christ's parables are often about patience: the barren fig-tree (*Lk* 13:6–9) – give it another year, look after it better and perhaps it will bear fruit; the prodigal son, tirelessly awaited by his father; the merciless servant (*Mt* 18:23) who had already been treated merciful'y himself.

In his Passion, Jesus joins the long line of sufferers, of those persecuted for righteousness' sake, for the sake of the Word of God. He is being persecuted, he says, by 'the sons of the people who murdered the prophets. Very well, finish off the work that your forefathers began!' (*Mt* 23:31). God's patience involves much waiting, but it entails suffering too. 'Son though he was, he learned to obey by suffering' (*Heb* 5:8) and he was 'obedient, even to the point of dying, of dying on a cross' (*Ph* 2:8). Jesus knew that his Passion was mysteriously necessary. 'Wasn't it necessary,' he said to the disciples on the way to Emmaus, 'for this Christ to suffer, to enter his glory?' (*Lk* 24:26). All this is God's patience made visible. Jesus is 'familiar with suffering' (*Is* 53:3), with betrayal by Judas, with denial by Peter, with apparent desertion by God. Christ's patience should pass into us – we shall say more about this. Lent is a season for meditating on this particular patience which we call 'passion'. Christ's Passion is the instrument to break down the barriers of our hearts.

How are we to model ourselves on the patience of God, on the patience of Jesus? In trying to do this, we shall find two kinds of patience are necessary. The first is needed as we contemplate the scandals of our times and the delays in the fulfilment of the kingdom and the Second Coming of the Lord. 'Why, O Lord, why all these delays? Why are you so long about righting the wrongs of the oppressed? The delays are themselves the continuation of God's Old Testament patience into our own times. God still goes on being patient. The apostle Peter tells us why: 'There is one thing in any case, my friends, that you must not forget: that with the Lord "a day" can mean a thousand years, and a thousand years is like a day. The Lord is not being slow about keeping his promise, although some people may say so, but he is being patient with you all, not wanting anyone to perish, but all to be converted.' He is waiting for our conversion, for the measure to be heaped up and completely full. 'And remind yourselves that the Lord's long patience is your opportunity for being saved. Paul who was so dear to us told you this when he wrote to you with that wisdom which is his special gift' (2 *P* 3:8–9, 15).

The second kind of patience is that required of our stature as Christians; it is indeed part of our nature, since 'we are children of God. Children, hence heirs, heirs of God and co-heirs with Christ, sharing Christ's suffering, so as to share his glory' (*Rm* 8:17). Thus, patience entails suffering and is itself an ordeal. 'So be patient, brothers, until the Lord's coming. Think of a farmer: patiently he waits for the precious fruit of the soil, until it has had the autumn rains and the spring rains! You too have to be patient: do not lose heart, for the Lord's coming will be soon . . . For your example in suffering and patience, brothers, take the prophets who spoke in the name of the Lord. Remember: those who had endurance are the ones that we call the blessed. You have heard the story of Job's patience and understood the Lord's purpose, realising that the Lord is kind and compassionate' (*Jm* 5:7–8, 10–11). And again, 'Brothers, treat your trials when they come as a happy privilege, knowing that your faith is only put to the test to make you patient' (*Jm* 1:2–3).

We see how very frequently these words, patience, suffering and constancy recur: Paul and Barnabas warned their converts, to save them from losing heart: 'They put fresh heart into the disciples, encouraging them to persevere in the faith, "for", said they, "we all have to experience many hardships before we enter the Kingdom of God" (*Ac* 14:22). And Paul was to repeat this to the Thessalonians, 'Let Timothy keep you firm, so that no one be unsettled by the present troubles; for as you know, these are bound to come our way. When we

were with you, we warned you that we must expect to have
ordeals to bear; and this is what has happened now, as you
have found out' (1 *Th* 3:2–4).

Experiencing ordeals, in Paul's view, is the normal condition for Christians until the final coming of Christ. For the
words patience, constancy and endurance are the co-relatives
of these other words: ordeal, distress, tribulation. This is
what Jesus tells us: 'I have told you all this so that you may
find peace in me. In the world you will have to suffer. But
be brave! I have conquered the world' (*Jn* 16:33). The *Epistle
to the Hebrews* describes the way in which Christ's victory was
won: 'With so many witnesses in a great cloud on every side of
us, we too, then, should throw off everything that hinders us,
especially the sin that clings so easily, and keep running
steadily in the race we have started. Let us not lose sight of
Jesus, who leads us in our faith and brings it to perfection; for
the sake of the joy which was still in the future, he endured the
cross, disregarding the shamefulness of it, and from now on
has taken his place at the right side of God's throne. Think of
the way he stood such opposition from sinners and then you
will not give up for want of courage. In the fight against sin,
you have not yet had to keep fighting to the point of death'
(12:1–4). We see this: Christ is 'destined to be a sign that is
rejected', as the aged Simeon prophesied to the Child's
Mother in the Temple. If we look at Christ, we shall see that
he is the ground in which patience and perseverance have
their roots.

What we have been saying so far represents the harsher
aspect of these words, and, if we do not experience this for
ourselves, we are in the path of delusion. But just as vigorously
and just as joyously, we have to hold on to their connotations
of light and of ultimate certainty. A chain-reaction takes
place; all these tribulations, trials and occasions for patience
and constancy, St. Paul explains, culminate in faith. 'We can
boast about our sufferings; for these sufferings bring patience,
as we know, and patience brings perseverance, and
perseverance brings hope, and this hope is not deceptive,
because God's love has been poured into our hearts by the
Holy Spirit' (*Rm* 5:3–5).

And thus we have a great certainty. Something immense is stored up in the grain of corn, thrown on the ground where it dies – to bear fruit and not remain alone. These ordeals bring us to the fountains of living water; they clear the ground of obstructions. Here is what St. Peter says about them: 'My dear people, you must not think it unaccountable that you should be tested by fire. There is nothing extraordinary in what has happened to you. If you can have some share in the sufferings of Christ, be glad, because you will enjoy a much greater gladness when his glory is revealed. It is a blessing for you when they insult you for bearing the name of Christ, because it means that you have the Spirit of Glory resting on you' (1 *P* 4:12–14). And a little further on, the apostle says: 'Stand up to Satan, strong in faith and in the knowledge that your brothers all over the world are suffering the same things. You will have to suffer only for a little while: the God of all grace who called you to eternal glory in Christ will see that all is well again: he will confirm you, strengthen you and support you' (5:9–10).

So here we are, ever in tension, as St. Paul says, between 'troubles which are soon over and which, though they weigh little, train us for carrying a weight of eternal glory which is out of all proportion to them' (2 *Co* 4:17, *Rm* 8:18).

Jacob's Strife

This is all true, we feel, we know, but isn't it a bit too tough for us? Is it really within our scope? For answer, I suggest that you look at Jacob and make friends with him. For a long time I never felt very keen on Jacob; a trickster, a cheat, a schemer, the supplanter of his elder brother. Not that Esau seemed much better, and a bit dim-witted into the bargain. Even so, Jacob was going rather far when he stole the blessing from bleary-eyed old Isaac. Later, he made a fortune at his father--in-law's expense in pretty sly transactions over sheep. Finally, having some twenty years later made his peace with Esau, he staves him off with lengthy greetings and elaborate presents until he has successfully parked the greater part of his possessions out of harm's way. Jacob depends on his own well-oiled tongue to get him out of scrapes. This is quite true.

But it is equally true that Jacob is often cheated too. He gets Isaac's blessing but has to flee at top speed, since Esau swears to have his guts as soon as the old man is dead: 'The time to mourn for my father will soon be here, and then I shall kill my brother Jacob.' There wouldn't be long to wait. Jacob is also cheated by his father-in-law, when, on his wedding-morning, he wakes up with Leah, instead of Rachel, in his arms. According to an amusing fourth-century Jewish homily, Jacob says to Leah: 'Artful hussy, why have you deceived me?' Leah replies, 'What about you? Why did you deceive your father when he said, "Are you really my son Esau?" ' So Jacob only got what he deserved. Exploited by his father-in-law who made him work for two seven-year stints and six years extra, he was to experience other hard knocks too: first, Rachel's childlessness, next the rape of his daughter Dinah, then the loss of his favourite son Joseph, followed by that of Simeon and Benjamin. So the all-too-human Jacob is not so unlike us. Abraham and Moses are too great, but in Jacob we can easily see ourselves.

If, however, we look at him from above, from God's point of view, we see that the fact over-riding Jacob's artfulness and his expiations is that he is doubly father of Israel. He is, first of all, by blood and his twelve sons, the ancestor of the twelve tribes. But the people of the twelve tribes also take their name from him: that name, Israel, which he himself received from God. Father twice over: once by blood, once by name. Jewish tradition makes a point of emphasising Jacob's greatness: it sees him as the man who chose the world to come, as opposed to Esau who chose the immediate one. Esau was tired, he was hungry, he asked for some lentil stew, later he married foreign wives. The Bible calls him the 'Misprizer', because he misprized the birthright bestowed on him by God, which would have made him the recipient of the Promise.

For us, Jacob is the man whose vision and struggle light up our own spiritual warfare. We are the children of the man who overcame God: Israel, 'he who fought with God'. Jacob's whole life is sandwiched between two encounters with God,

takes place as it were between two meetings: the dream at
Bethel and the fight at the ford of the Jabbok. Twenty years
separate these two moments. Both incidents occur at a time of
ordeal, and at night. Both times, Jacob is alone and both
times, in a state of stress. The first time, he is running away,
alone, with only his staff, and he has six hundred miles to
cover before reaching his distant relatives and finding a wife.
The second time, he is on his way to meet Esau and the latter
is barring his way with four hundred armed men.

The first encounter was that mysterious dream, dreamt by
someone seemingly quite unworthy of being God's man, and
yet who became precisely that. St. Paul says: 'If God is with
us, who can be against us?' I should be inclined to say, 'If
Jacob was chosen by God, why shouldn't I be?' We are people
of the same kidney. Quite unworthy.

Jacob is on his way to Haran. It is evening on one of the
earliest stages of his journey. The sun goes down. He takes one
of the stones lying about, puts it under his head and falls
asleep. He dreams: and sees a ladder pitched on earth with its
top reaching to heaven; the angels of God are going up and
down on it. 'And there was Yahweh standing beside him, saying, "I Yahweh am the God of your forefather Abraham and
the God of Isaac . . . I am with you. I shall keep you safe
wherever you go" (*Gn* 28:13, 15). So Jacob is not alone after
all. God is taking care of him, is with him, will not abandon
him. The invisible becomes visible in the ordeal. Cardinal
Newman's comment on this episode is good:

'Jacob little thought that there was anything marvellous in
this place. It was a place like any other, it was lonely and com-
fortless. There was no house. Night came and he had to sleep
on the bare rock. And yet, how different was the reality! He
only saw the visible world, and yet the invisible was there!'

This is what we learn from Jacob's dream: God is there.
And God speaks to him. At the top of the ladder is God. But
the text says much more: Yahweh was standing beside him
while he was asleep. God is not only at the top of the ladder,
but actually standing beside him. It wasn't the angels who
came down to Jacob, but God himself. The God who is entirely other, the Almighty, these angels going up and coming

down, this kind of alternating current, this funicular railway (if you'll allow the term), is truly God-with-us coming to Jacob. A spiritual revolution is taking place and we should focus our attention very sharply on it.

For people of those days, for all peoples, even the most advanced, there was no constant link with God. God was not interested in men. God might come, but as destiny, as fate, as the God of the philosophers, – not as a God talking as man to man with one of his creatures and 'standing beside him'. With Jacob, we see a mysterious but real bond of union between creature and Creator, a current of grace – and this was not the result of a sacrifice by which Jacob had given something to God in the first place. It didn't even arise out of a convenantal pact. No. Here we are talking about friendship. Contrast the Tower of Babel with its top intended to pierce the heavens (arrogance) and the ladder pitched on earth with the top leaning against the sky: and God is the one to take the initiative and come down. In the case of the Tower of Babel, man is trying to do something; in Jacob's dream, grace is doing something. In the one case, man's presumption is at work; in the other, God's mercy – achieving what man's presumption never could achieve. In the one case, God is a rival, sin is committed, discord ensues; in the other, God is Father, he admits man into a covenant with him, admits him into his own life. The angels go up and come down. Later, Jesus was to say to Nathaneal, 'I tell you most solemnly, you will see heaven laid open and, above the Son of Man, the angels of God ascending and descending' (*Jn* 1:51). Jesus was to be the true Ladder, when 'raised' on the cross.

And God, at the same time as revealing his presence to Jacob, renews his covenant with him: 'I Yahweh am the God of your forefather Abraham and the God of Isaac. The ground on which you are resting I shall give to you and your descendants. Your descendants will be as plentiful as dust on the ground, and you will spread out west and east, and north and south.' Here is the splendour and the end of tribulation. 'All the communities of the earth will bless themselves by you and your descendants. Be sure, I am with you; I shall keep you safe wherever you go, and bring you back to this country; for I

shall not desert you before doing what I have promised you.'
Jacob wakes up from his sleep and says, 'Truly, Yahweh
resides in this place and I never knew it.' And of this God,
making Jacob a present of the future, the great Jewish mystic
Bahya ibn Paquda makes the point: 'of this God, crowning
Jacob's head with stars, all Jacob asks is a bit of bread to eat
and some clothes to wear, and all the rest he leaves to God's
goodness.'

This is the noble view – and perfectly justified. On the other
hand, in what Jacob actually said there were a fair number of
rather embarrassing 'ifs': '*If* God stays with me . . . *if* he keeps
me safe on this journey . . . *if* he gives me bread to eat . . . *if* he
gives me clothes to wear and I come back, Yahweh shall be my
God.' Not a total conversion yet, perhaps. God promises him,
'I shall give you everything.' Jacob, for his part, still has a few
conditions to make.

Twenty years later, the conversion is complete. The last
battle. Jacob is on his way home and reaches the ford on the
Jabbok. Twenty years, and God has fulfilled his promise. The
vagabond of Bethel comes home a patriarch. He has flocks,
children. It now remains for him to go through the redoubtable ordeal of middle age. Before, when he passed this spot,
he had everything to win. All he owned was his staff. This
time, he has everything to lose. And grace, at this moment,
will take the form of fear: his anguish before confronting Esau.
So Jacob prays. For the first time, he prays properly, not making too much of his own remarkable traits of character, 'O
God of my forefather Abraham and God of my father Isaac, O
Yahweh who told me, "Go back to your native land and I will
be good to you,", I am unworthy of all the kindness which you
have steadfastly shown your servant.' Jacob abases himself.
For the first time, he has hit rock-bottom, has reached the end
of his tether. Up to this point, he had supposed that his wits
would carry him through, he had tried out all his diplomatic
wiles on Esau; now, he is alone. And now, Jacob prepares to
confront a man, his brother, over whom trickery and charm
may yet win the day. He prepares to meet his brother's anger
and the four hundred armed men now on their way, but what

is really terrifying is not his brother or his brother's
henchmen, but God's anger. What has to be overcome is not
material obstacle, war, illness or death, but God's opposition.
God who 'when he opens, no one can shut; and when he shuts,
no one can open'. And God it is who intervenes, just when
Jacob has only got this last trickle of water to cross.

This may not be immediately easy to grasp! Behind the circumstances, the things, the men, the dangers, the fortunate or
unfortunate accidents, the efforts and the labours, God is the
one with whom Jacob has to deal, God alone, God in person.
All the other things are merely visible clues to the designs of
the invisible God. And the hidden God irrupts this time, not in
a dream, but in a fight.

Jacob stays behind on his own. A man wrestles with him
until daybreak. The man realises that he cannot beat Jacob;
he strikes him on the hip and in the ensuing struggle Jacob's
hip is wrenched out of its socket. 'The unknown man says,
"Let me go, for it is daybreak." "I will not let you go, unless
you bless me!" Said the other, "What is your name?" He
replied, "Jacob." Said he, "You shall no longer be spoken of
as Jacob but as Israel, for you have striven with beings divine
and human, and have won." Jacob then asked, "Please tell
me *your* name." He replied, "You must not ask *my* name."
With that, he blessed him.'

Who was the man? Who was it who opposed Jacob's return
to the Promised Land? Who was trying to kill him? Jacob was
alone, as we always are in the ordeals of desertion, illness and
death. Jacob's great struggle is every man's final struggle. –
And God himself said, 'You have been struggling with God';
you have not been wrestling with merely immediate
difficulties, but with God himself. Jacob exclaims, ' I have
seen God face to face!' But what an interview! A hand--
to-hand battle lasting throughout the night, both of them rolling in the dust. This isn't a game of make-believe; this isn't
any fun at all. Jacob doesn't say, 'Your will be done.' He
wrestles till dawn. Can it be, in some incredible way, that
Jacob is stronger than God? Not possible – or God wouldn't
be God any more. Then where does Jacob get the strength to
fight all night and still not be beaten by his opponent? Jacob

fights – this is what we discover – with God's own weapons. For arms, Jacob defends himself with God's promise and God's fidelity to his promise. Like Job, when he says, 'Yea, though he kill me, yet will I trust in·him'; like Teresa of the Child Jesus, thousands of years later. All the while you hope, you are not beaten. Jacob wins, by hope. 'Hold on to love and justice, and hope in your God always,' says Hosea. Jacob's strength lies in his hope, no longer in his wits, in his own efforts or in his own resources. 'Since you have promised it' – this is Jacob's only weapon – not even God can conquer him. *Wisdom* was to say of Jacob: 'In an arduous struggle, she awarded him the prize, to teach him that piety is stronger than all' (*Ws* 10:12). And at dawn he receives the name Israel: 'Strong in striving with God and with men.'

Note the symbolism of this name, to pass from Jacob to the nation. He is the man who clings to God as someone clings in a wrestling match; the man who, by God's mercy, can make some of God's strength his own by hope, and who forces God to protect him, since he goes on fighting 'to the end', as Jesus did. And indeed, at this moment, God does show himself to be weaker than man, since God's weakness lies in his respect for our freedom.

You could say, with Père M. D. Molinié: 'God's love for us, like all great love, is at once timid and totalitarian.' These are human expressions, but they contain a lot of truth. A God who loves becomes timid since, although wanting all, giving all and demanding all, he waits for us to give it freely and willingly. The greatest danger for Jacob would have been to *stop* fighting or, to use a military expression, 'to have broken off the engagement'. Jacob emerged the victor because God had already said to him at Bethel, 'I am with you, wherever you go.' Even when God was fighting Jacob, he could not really be *against* him, or he would have been breaking his promise to be *with* him. This is what the monk Gueric of Igny said in one of his sermons:

'O Goodness full of artifice, disguising yourself in harshness! How lovingly you fight against those for whom you fight! . . . So do not lose hope, but stand firm, O fortunate soul already engaged in struggling with God. Yes, he wants you to wound him, he longs for you to defeat him. Indeed, even when he is angry and stretches out his hand to strike, he seeks – he has said so himself – a man like Moses, who will stand up to him. And if he cannot find one, he complains, "There is no one to stand up and restrain me." '

Until the crack of dawn, when God is obliged to leave so that Jacob will not see his face, God is the prisoner of his own fidelity. And of Jacob it is required that he too stand firm in the darkness until dawn. Jesus made this the rule for his disciples: 'He who stands firm to the end, will be saved,' – he who has fought with God and not been beaten. This is the ultimate and overwhelming proof of God's fidelity.

Thus, having said and sung, 'Yes, you are a faithful God', man has to go through the ordeal of proving God's fidelity in single combat. Our conviction that God is God, that he loves us and that he cannot abandon us, is put to the proof and demonstrated in a hand-to-hand struggle. And no quarter given! And indeed, this is exactly what St. Paul tells us: 'Grow strong in the Lord and in the strength of his power.' – You are going to fight a battle, but will have God's strength to win it. – 'Put God's armour on,' – not your own, not Goliath's – 'so as to be able to resist the tactics of the Devil. For not against human enemies have we got to struggle' – all those things of human origin, which are themselves real enough, but beyond them – 'against the Sovereignties and Powers who originate the darkness in this world, the spiritual army of Evil. That is why you must rely on God's armour, so as to put up a resistance when the worst happens and, having used all these resources, to stand firm' (*Ep* 6:10–17).

We shall come across these austere words again, but rephrased this time into a victory hymn: 'So stand your ground, with truth buckled round your waist' – Christ said: 'I am the Truth, the Life' – 'and integrity for a breastplate, wearing for shoes the eagerness to spread the gospel of peace, and always carrying the shield of faith so that you can use it to put out the Evil One's burning arrows; and then you must accept the helmet of salvation and the sword of the Spirit' – the double-edged sword – 'that is to say, the Word of God'. And St. Paul adds, since prayer and battle are inseparable:

'Pray all the time, asking for what you need, praying in the Spirit on every possible occasion' (*Ep* 6:18).

We are all called to fight Jacob's battle. 'Don't be afraid. I have conquered the world' – because I have wrestled with God – as Jesus did that night in Gethsemane.

MOSES

From adoration to intercession

After Abraham, the pioneer of prayer, and Jacob who wrestled with God, we come to Moses. Abraham was the Christopher Columbus of blind faith: the man who, at a word, set out for an unknown country and an unknown future. Abraham set out, relying on the fragile evidence of an inner message, but in pure and absolute trust nonetheless. He went forward, although there was no road. In prayer, there is always an element of Abraham: prayer is always a departure into the unknown, an act of trust.

Moses was the man to whom the actual content of faith was revealed, and revealed by God in person. Abraham had set out with no mapped route, across a desert, making for a country to which God merely indicated the direction from day to day: 'the country which I shall show you'. To Moses, however, God gave the material for building the road; he gave him the Torah, which we translate – badly – as the Law. 'For the Torah, in Hebrew,' says the great Jewish writer André Neher, 'is not the order but the orientation, not the law but the way, the route along which a community can travel.' The word Torah hence evokes a road, a route to follow, not only for the individual but for a whole people. 'Walk in my way,' is the constant refrain of the Old Testament, and Christ's disciples came to be known as the Disciples of the Way (*Ac* 18:25).

With Moses, as with Abraham, God sealed a Covenant. The essence of the Covenant with Abraham was the promise to create a people, of a new relationship with God ('I shall be your God') and of ownership of a country. To cement this covenant, God asked Abraham 'to walk in his presence' and to make the divine gifts his by performing a symbolic action: cir-

cumcision. But this was still only a promise, to which
Abraham had to cling by faith. Israel did not properly become
Yahweh's people until the revelation of the Torah; that is to
say, God's covenant with Moses on Mount Sinai.

In this Covenant, God revealed a hitherto unknown and unimaginable secret to Moses: God draws near to man, makes
friends with him, binds himself to man by contract to lead him
to the country promised long ago to Abraham, the 'restful
place' which in fact proves to be nothing less than God
himself, than life with him.

When St. Paul speaks of the 'mystery hidden throughout
the centuries and revealed in Jesus Christ', he is speaking of
the New Covenant made by Jesus, no longer with an individual people, but with the whole human race. But the covenant with Moses is already the first step towards this final
revelation.

The four books of the Pentateuch which deal with Moses
show him as a man of prayer, of prayer taking diverse forms
but consistent and incessant. Moses is the contemplative
launched into the world of action; and the contemplative in
action is the apostle, the prophet. Moses is the exemplar of all
the Old Testament prophets, and God himself accorded him
the title (*Dt* 18:15, 34:10), the greatest prophet until John the
Baptist, who in Christ's words was in any case 'more than a
prophet'.

By his life, Moses teaches us three attitudes appropriate to
man before his God, three forms of, and three truths about,
prayer. Moses is the man of adoration, the man of intercession
and action, and the man of praise.

Adoration

Moses was alone, on the far side of the wilderness, near
Mount Horeb, pasturing his father-in-law's flocks. He had
fled from Egypt a long time before (*Ex* 2:23). Stephen in the
Acts of the Apostles was to say, 'forty years having gone by', by
which he meant that a new period in Moses's life was about to
begin. Doubtless though, and despite the passage of time, the

memory of his brothers, 'groaning' down in Egypt, for whose sake he had suffered and because of whom he was then in exile, haunted him in his solitude, in his desert refuge. To all human appearances, his exile was hopeless, just as the groans of the Israelites were hopeless; who was he, as opposed to Pharaoh? And so far away!

Then, as ever, as with Abraham, God takes the initiative, God intervenes. God always calls first. So does Jesus: 'I have chosen you,' and 'he called those whom he wanted to him'.

The Angel of Yahweh appeared to him in a fiery flame, from the middle of a bush. Moses looked: there was the bush blazing, but it was not being burnt (*Ex* 3:2).

Moses's first vision, like St. Paul's, begins with something strange, something different from the normal; a change, you might say, of gear. Consider Isaiah, whose lips were purified by the seraph with a live coal while the Temple was full of smoke; or St. Paul, blinded by the light on the road to Damascus. There is always a departure from the norm. Prayerful approach to God, even in daily prayer, should always be preceded by such a change.

'When Moses saw the bush ablaze but not being burnt, he said, "I must turn off and look at this strange sight" ' (*Ex* 3:2).

'Turn off!' Leave the road! Not leave it for good: but if we mean to enter prayer, we have to turn from the road. Jesus says, you must shut yourself in your bedroom. I am not saying that to pray you have to cut yourself off from life. Far from it! When Moses turned off the road, this did not cut him off from life – far from it! And the roundabout route of the Exodus will confirm this. Even so, there is an initial turning-aside. And this turning-aside – note this – the Bible tells us that God 'sees' it. Yahweh saw that he had turned off. God 'sees' the changes of direction which we make in our efforts to approach him. And immediately, 'God called to him from the middle of the bush, "Moses! Moses!" – "Here I am," he replied.'

"Here I am." This is Abraham's response to God's call before the sacrifice of Isaac. It will be Mary's too. It is the only attitude by which we can enter prayer: that of an attentive heart. Moses's heart is ready to respond to God's first call. And yet:

'Come no nearer! Take off your sandals, for the place where you are standing is holy ground' (*Ex* 3:5). That is to say: leave your dust and dirt outside. Prayer must also be preceded by a period of settlement. When water has been disturbed, it gradually becomes clear again if you leave it to stand. The slime and impurities sink to the bottom. To prayer, which is a gift from God, we must bring a limpid and undisturbed heart. That is why prayer must last for a certain length of time, time in which to become un-disturbed. We know the feeling well: there are days or times when even after half an hour we have hardly begun to settle down. The first half-hour is nothing but inner disturbance, be our goodwill what it may. This is why three separate quarters of an hour can never add up to three quarters of an hour at a stretch: there is hardly time to stop being disturbed. Possibly, when some Carthusian turns the switch, prayer comes instantly. Possibly! But whatever sort of life you lead, the human heart, of its nature, is never entirely undisturbed.

Cardinal Mercier used to say: 'I am going to tell you one of the secrets of holiness and happiness: every day, for a few seconds, learn to silence your imagination, to close your eyes to visible things and your ears to noise, to go into yourself' – 'take off your sandals' – and there, in the sanctuary of your soul, which is the Temple of the Holy Spirit, speak to the Spirit.'

When Jesus spoke about prayer, he said only one thing: 'Persevere!' He never said, 'Let your prayer be gentle, peaceful or this or that,' but simply, 'Persevere!' Where there is continuity, settlement takes place.

So the first attitude to prepare for adoration: I turn aside to listen, and I take off my sandals to approach Him. God himself tells us to do this. We do not approach him with impunity, nor just anyhow. Moses's adoration is not undisciplined and wild.

Then this God, invisible yet present in the form of a fiery flame, reveals himself to Moses: 'I am the God of your forefather, the God of Abraham, the God of Isaac and the God of Jacob.' And immediately afterwards, as Moses covers his face: 'I have seen, I have seen the miserable state of my people.

Now go! I am sending you.'

'I have seen,' says God. Like Moses in exile, man supposes himself to be alone: he thinks, he remembers, he worries, he suffers. Alone. That is a state which we are often in. We do not know – or we no longer remember – that God is there.

'God was there and I never knew it!' This was Jacob's great discovery, made again by Moses at the burning bush – one which we must keep making over and over again. And Moses, at God's first summons, answered, 'Here I am!' Then God shows how close he is and that he too, just as much as Moses, remembers the misery of his people.

'I am the God of your forefather.' Having shown Moses that he was the Holy One, the Entirely Other, God wants to come quite close, in a way to approach Moses, to have Moses recognise him. 'To this man of the tribe of Levi, the God of the Forefathers reveals himself in perfect conformity to a long tradition,' writes Neher. As background to the story, there is a general familiarity with this God, adored and known for many generations (Abraham, Isaac, Jacob). Other generations have perhaps forgotten him during those years of slavery; even so, God does not hesitate to introduce himself to Moses as 'the God of your forefather'. The memory of the patriarchs was still very much alive.

'Now go! . . . I am sending you.' Moses answers, 'Very well. I shall go back to the Israelites and say to them, "The God of your forefathers has sent me to you." But if they ask me what his name is, what shall I tell them?'

The Divine Name

Then, as to Abraham, but much more completely than to Abraham, the Divine Name is given to Moses. To Abraham, God gave his name as El Shaddai (God the Mountain-dweller). And to Abraham, in his long life of travelling in the presence, El Shaddai became to such a degree his Lord and his God, that to Moses God presents himself as 'Abraham's God'.

But Moses wants to know his forefather's God more personally; he wants this knowledge for himself and for his brothers. At this point, Moses indeed begins to pray. True, God calls and begins the conversation first, but conversation can only be carried on if man desires it too. God respects man's deepest wishes. God doesn't reveal his name of his own accord, so to speak. He waits until someone wants to know him, until someone comes looking for him. Then God said to Moses, 'I AM WHO I AM'.

This revelation of the Name of Yahweh is in response to Moses's desire, and it is a proper response, not a conundrum. But God nonetheless is the Unnameable, Indefinable One; hence, the Divine Name is at once a revelation of God and a revelation of the mystery of God. God reveals himself, unveils himself in his Name, even though the Name is still mysterious. There are several possible translations, each throwing light on this unfathomable Name: 'I am who I am', or 'I shall be who I shall be', or 'I am here'.

So prayer means opening our mind or, more exactly, letting the Divine Name open our mind and heart to the true scale of values: the transcendance of God, before which we become aware of our own limitations, and the summons from God bidding us overcome those limitations and go to meet him. We have to realise our limitations and accept them, and at the same time be impatient to go beyond them. Prayer is this constant oscillation of the heart.

Conversation: You and I

Henceforward, a constant conversation takes place between Yahweh and Moses. The latter sets off across the wilderness 'with the staff of God'. Throughout the long road, simultaneously beset·by marvels and difficulties, eventually leading Moses to Sinai, he becomes more and more intimate with God, never wanting the divine presence to leave him. Moses never stops praying, imploring, even insisting – like the importunate friend in the Gospel – and his entire prayer, like Abraham's, depends henceforth and exclusively on the very word of God: 'You yourself said to me . . . but . . .' (*Ex* 33:12).

The greatness of Moses did not lie in his God-given strength to conquer Pharaoh or to lead the people through their host of difficulties; nor even in being a prophet. His greatness lay in having a heart which loved his Lord more than all the gifts which he had received from him. It lay in being by disposition of heart and not merely by virtue of the mission received, 'the servant of Yahweh'. And the greatness of Moses is defined by God himself, who tells us (*Nb* 12:6–8):

If any man among you is a prophet,
I make myself known to him in a vision,
I speak to him in a dream.
Not so with my servant Moses:
he is at home in my house;
I speak to him face to face,
plainly and not in riddles,
and he sees Yahweh's Glory.

The greatness of Moses lies in his intimacy with his Lord. Given that Moses was at home in God's house as 'faithful servant', Jesus for his part was at home there, the *Epistle to the Hebrews* tells us, as 'faithful son'. And through prayer, not only *through* prayer but *primarily* through prayer, we too ought to be 'at home in God's house as sons' (*Heb* 3:2–5).

We see the intimacy of Moses with his God in another passage, in *Exodus*. This is when the covenant is being made. Here is the impressive preparation for the climax: 'Moses went up the mountain. The cloud covered the mountain, and the Glory of Yahweh settled on Mount Sinai. For six days, the cloud covered it and on the seventh day Yahweh called to Moses from inside the cloud. To the eyes of the children of Israel, the Glory of Yahweh seemed like a devouring fire on the mountain top. Moses went into the cloud. He went up the mountain, and stayed there for forty days and forty nights' (*Ex* 24:15–18).

Moses, we observe, waited for six days. God only called to him on the seventh. Six days at God's disposal. Moses goes deeper and deeper into the cloud, he climbs higher and higher up the mountain (we never stop climbing up the Mountain of

God); he has to stay there for forty days and forty nights (no quarter-hour stints for him!) The Bible passes over the forty-days conversation in respectful silence.

And this is followed by the account of the astonishing intimacy which developed out of this dialogue on the mountain. Perhaps we have read it too often to feel its full impact. 'Moses used to take the Tent of Meeting and set it up for him, outside the camp, at some distance from the camp,' where his prevaricating people lived, and 'the pillar of cloud would come down and station itself at the entrance to the Tent, and Yahweh would talk to Moses . . . Yahweh would talk to Moses as a man talks to his friend' (*Ex* 33:7–11).

It is impossible to go further in the prayer of adoration than this. God is not a God whose transcendance overwhelms us and requires us to grovel before him, but a God who talks to us as a man talks to his friend. Here, what Jesus says, was already true for Moses: 'From now on, I shall not call you servants, but friends.'

In *Moise et la Vocation juive* (Moses and the Vocation of the Jews), written after the massacres at Auschwitz and elsewhere, and all the more impressive since the author is himself a Jew, André Neher sums up the character of Moses like this: 'Moses is the man of the First Commandment, the man whom God seeks out, singles out and seizes: "I am your God"'.

The word due for emphasis is 'your'. God doesn't merely tell Moses, 'I am God'; he says, 'I am your God.' But the point is, as Neher observes, 'Moses does not take "your" (singular in Hebrew) as applying to himself as an individual; he understands it as God's Word spoken once for all to the Jewish people.' Moses, as we shall see, never thought of dissociating himself from the people as a whole; quite the reverse. He himself accepted responsibility whenever the people complained or fell short of the trust in God that God required of them. Moses as first recipient of the personal message 'your God', lived out the message as individual and people – just as Mary was able to be simultaneously herself and the whole Church. In Moses, the personal and collective message were identical from the first instant of revelation on Sinai. From

a quasi-"corporate"-personhood

him, beginning with him, the conviction of a personal God –
gradually, very slowly, despite a great number of stiff necks! –
gradually spread to everyone.

From the moment that Moses met Yahweh in the burning
bush, he ceased to be alone. 'He was never on his own,' Neher
says. And prayer should be like this. Having recognised the
God of his forefathers in Yahweh and having later made the
victorious crossing of the Sea of Reeds, Moses sang, 'He is my
God – I praise him.' God now becomes more and more intimate with him. God speaks to him as a friend: 'I am your
God.'

I am your God, he is my God. Prayer is between *you* and *me*:
a loving conversation. 'Today God converses lovingly with
you, and today you converse lovingly with God' (*Dt*
26:17–18). Even though misconceived piety may have
obscured this primal truth, it is true all the same. And this is
why God speaks of himself as 'a devouring fire', a 'jealous
God', for his love, being so intense, leads to this jealousy.

Knowing God = gift of the Name + conversation

The giving of the Divine Name, conversing with God, the
you-and-me relationship with God, leads to ever-growing ac-
quaintance with God and a desire to know him even better.
Prayer is the acceleration of this desire to know God.

A thirst for God is born in Moses; in the midst of his labours
– and in this marvellous respect he is our master – Moses is
forever seeking the face of God, of the God whose favour he
has won and who knows him by name (*Ex* 33:12–17).

Thirstier and thirstier for knowledge of his Lord, Moses
becomes bolder in prayer: 'Please allow me to see your glory.'
On earth, there is no greater desire that man can have than to
share in this divine intimacy; and our nobility as man resides
in the purity and strength of this desire. By it, man recovers
his likeness to God. To see God is to become like him: 'We
shall be like him, because we shall see him as he really is' (1 *Jn*
3:2). Every aspiration of mankind, not only of the believer, but
every aspiration of modern man to know himself and the

marvels of the world in which he lives, is a repetition, however deformed and unenlightened, of this very prayer: 'Please allow me to see your glory.'

Your glory – your splendour in all its radiance. Show yourself, my God, as you really are and not as I diminish you. In another manuscript of *Exodus* it says: 'Show yourself to me.' We see how Moses's perpetual desire makes him more and more aware of God's transcendant greatness. 'Make yourself known!' This is a long way from contemplating our own navels!

And God hears his request: 'I shall cause my whole splendour to pass before you, and in front of you I shall utter the name Yahweh' (*Ex* 33:19). The name which you so desire to know, you shall hear from the very mouth of God; not only will you see his splendour, but you will know the name. You will know the incomparable riches of his Name. This is the great revelation: not only the giving of the name but developing, or rather 'dis-enveloping' everything contained in that name: tenderness, pity, love, favour, fidelity.

'But you cannot see my face, for man cannot see my face and live.' The tension of prayer lies in hearing God simultaneously say: 'I shall pass in front of you' and 'You cannot see my face.' All the same, Yahweh hears Moses's prayer: 'Here is a place beside me. You are to stand on the rock. And when my Glory goes by, I shall put you in a cleft in the rock and shield you with my hand as I pass by. Then I shall take my hand away and you will see my back, but my face cannot be seen' (*Ex* 33:21).

Moses's desire to see God is heard: the back, admittedly, but it is God all the same. This is a perfect description of the mechanics of the meeting with God and of what causes our thirst for God. He is there, but we only see him imperfectly, 'dimly,' as St. Paul says, 'as in a mirror.' The desire to be face to face with him grows stronger in prayerful conversation, accelerated by our increasingly intimate knowledge of the Divine Name.

The amazing discovery

We think of the headlines in the popular press: Someone-or-
-other's secret sorrow ... Somebody else's appalling shock.
And what comes next we might call 'Moses's amazing discovery'. His amazing discovery was that man can love God.
That God can love man is amazing enough, but that man can
love God! Neher observes: 'That God loved man, that he was
their Father and protector, had already been suspected, if not
clearly expressed, by other religious geniuses of antiquity. But
that man should be invited to love God was something really
to shake the religious fabric of the world.' No longer only fear,
but love: this is the upshot of the covenant. 'Then Moses invoked the name of Yahweh. Yahweh passed before him and
shouted: "Yahweh, Yahweh, God of tenderness and compassion, slow to anger, rich in kindness and fidelity!"' (*Ex* 36:6).
    Everything that happens in the Bible is as though God were
only revealing his own need to love ('I am a jealous God')
because of his own need to be loved, because he is waiting to
be loved. Hence, prayer is not a tax paid to God, not a duty
which we have pledged ourselves to perform. Prayer is the loving search for God's face. Loving, of course, does not mean
that we are happy all the time while doing this. Oh no! But I
seek him, I go to him, I turn off my road, I draw near to him, I
want to know him. 'Yahweh spoke to Moses face to face in the
dark cloud, like a man talking to a friend.' Prayer, as with
Moses, consists in listening to God as he talks to me face to
face, like a friend talking to a friend. And if God talks to me
like this, this is how I shall talk to him.

Intercession

The prayer of adoration and the ensuing conversation lead us
to intercession. We have to get the order right: just as the first
great commandment is to love God, and just as the second, to
love our brother – which is no less important – has its origin in
the first, so intercession has its origin in adoration, and not the
other way round.

Let us go on studying the account of God's apparition to Moses: 'Yahweh, Yahweh, God of tenderness and compassion, slow to anger, rich in kindness' – hence the reason for intercession – 'maintaining his kindness to thousands and tolerating fault, transgression and sin, yet letting nothing go unchecked and punishing faults.' Immediately – here comes intercession – Moses threw himself on his knees and then prostrate on the ground. He then said, 'If I have indeed won your favour, Lord, deign, my Lord, to come with us. True, they are a stiff-necked people, but forgive us our faults and our sins, and adopt us as your heritage' (*Ex* 34:6–9). This is how adoration ('Let me see your Glory', 'I want to know you') merges into intercession.

'Lord, forgive, adopt us as your heritage'; this is a constant in the life of Moses. Adoration makes him the servant of his brothers and of his God. Adoration makes him both mediator and servant. God reveals his Name to him in the burning bush and says, 'Go and gather the elders of Israel together and tell them, "Yahweh has appeared to me" '. This is revelation and adoration combined. And then 'Go' – this 'go' is the very keynote of Moses's life: 'Go and tell Pharaoh', 'Go and find Pharaoh', 'Tell the Israelites to turn back', 'Tell the Israelites to set off again', 'Go and find the people and make them purify themselves', 'This is what you are to say to the Israelites', 'These are the laws which you are to give them'.

The neatest of the Devil's inventions over the past twenty years has been to insinuate that adoration is not part of living. How can anyone imagine that adoration of the Living God excludes us from living? It throws us further in! 'Go, you are to say, you are to do ... These are the laws you are to give.' Of course, adoration is nothing to do with living, if I am only adoring myself! But if our adoration is of God, that throws us back into living as nothing else can. As you can see from the accounts of how God's appearing to someone conditions that person's actual vocation:–

Isaiah – he sees the holiness of God. He becomes the servant and prophet of God's holiness.

Mary Magdalen – 'Mary!' – 'Rabbuni!' – 'Do not touch me. Go to my brothers.' God's word invariably throws us into life's turmoil as servants.

St. Paul – 'Go, you are one of my chosen instruments . . . and you will learn what you will have to suffer for my Name.'

God has no other way of doing things. Adoration leads to intercession. And each stage of Moses's life was punctuated, as you will see, by a prayer of intercession.

As soon as Moses goes back to Egypt and intervenes with Pharaoh, faced with the Pharaoh's demand for higher production and the people's consequent recriminations, Moses exclaims – and this is intercession – 'Lord, why?' Jesus was to say, 'Why have you forsaken me?' That is questioning in prayer.

The people are angry with Moses because the Egyptians are getting tougher with them. Moses doesn't say that he's not to blame; he forthwith turns to God. 'Lord,' he asks, 'why are you treating this people so harshly?'

The people grumble rebelliously in the salt-flats after crossing the Red Sea. Moses again calls to Yahweh and fresh water gushes from the rock. Moses intercedes.

Next there are rebellious mutterings from Miriam and Aaron! Moses's life was no fun, with his sister Miriam and his brother Aaron angry with him because he had taken a Cushite wife. 'Is Moses the only one whom Yahweh has spoken through? Hasn't he spoken through us too?' (*Nb* 12:2). Moses intercedes for them, in spite of their jealousy. But first, he keeps quiet, out of humility. And because of this, Yahweh himself takes up his defence.

And lastly, look at Moses's great act of intercession during the crucial battle with the Amalekites; this is the very model of intercession: 'Joshua followed Moses's instructions and took the field to engage Amalek. Moses, Aaron and Hur were on the top of the hill. As long as Moses kept his arms raised, Israel had the advantage; when he let his arms fall, the advantage went to Amalek' (*Ex* 17:10–14).

The efficacity of prayer and the vindication of contemplatives as against the active life could hardly be better demonstrated: 'As Moses's arms grew heavy, they took a stone and put it under him and on this he sat, Aaron and Hur supporting his arms, one on one side, one on the other. And so his arms remained firm till sunset.' If Moses chose prayer rather than the sword, it wasn't because he was lazy: 'Observing what labours he took on himself for the people's sake, Jethro said, "You will tire yourself out. The work is too heavy for you." ' (*Ex* 18:14, 18). And in this same passage we find a phrase exactly characterising his role as intercessor: 'You ought to represent the people before God and bring their disputes to him' (*Ex* 18:19).

Intercessory prayer is not platonic. After praying, the next thing you have to do is to plunge with all your weight into the hurly-burly of the evil-doers: not sit back and wash your hands! Gandhi, who would punish himself when his disciples did wrong was a wonderful example of this. Intercessory prayer can't end in hand-washing, like Pilate's. The episode of the Golden Calf shows the difference (*Ex* 32).

The incident of the Golden Calf begins like a household scene. 'Yahweh then said to Moses, "Go down now, for *your* people whom you brought out of Egypt have apostasised" ' (*Ex* 32:7). – You know, like when the wife says to her husband (or the other way round), 'Look what *your* son is doing now!' – ' "*Your* people have gone wrong. They haven't wasted any time in leaving the way. They have cast themselves a metal calf." Yahweh said to Moses, "I can see how stiff-necked these people are! Leave me now. My wrath is about to blaze out at them and I shall destroy them. I shall make a great nation of you instead." '

This is what God suggests to Moses: to dissociate himself from that stiff-necked people and himself, Moses, become a great nation. But Moses refuses and does his best to pacify Yahweh. Translated literally, it is even better: 'Moses sweetened the face of Yahweh' – intercessory prayer again – 'and said' – rather like Abraham with regard to Sodom – "Yahweh, why should your wrath blaze out at your people? Why let the Egyptians say, He brought them away out of spite, to make them perish in the mountains and wipe them off the face of the earth. – Leave your burning anger, relent and do not bring disaster on your people. Remember Abraham, Isaac and Jacob, your servants, to whom by your own self you swore and made this promise: I shall make your offspring as numerous as the stars of heaven" ' (*Ex* 32:11–13).

Moses is truly the beloved son who trusts his father and intercedes for his brothers. So God then says, 'Very well, go and find your people!' Moses goes. He is angry with them, reproaches them, tells them of the punishment in store. Like Jesus in the Temple, angry because it has been turned into a supermarket. Moses speaks to the people: 'You, all of you, have committed a great sin,' for now the intercessor is speaking from God's point of view. 'I was standing between God and you to tell you what Yahweh was saying' (*Dt* 5:5) – and he certainly has the courage to tell people the truth: 'I shall now go back up the mountain to Yahweh. Perhaps I can atone for your sin.' Then he goes back to Yahweh: 'Alas, this people has committed a great sin by making themselves a god of gold. And yet, if it pleased you to forgive their sin . . . ! If not, then blot me out of the book which you have written' (*Ex* 32:30, 32). Once more, Moses climbs the mountain to intercede, after the people's great sin. 'As before, I stayed on the mountain for forty days and forty nights. And this time too, God heard me and agreed not to destroy you' (*Dt* 10:10).

Adoration gives a man a true sense of values, but intercession springs from the depths of a sinful world.

Praise

Adoration plus intercession equals praise. Praise is adoration mingled with intercession – Biblical praise – since Biblical praise is rooted in life and events. Intercession without preliminary adoration equals bitterness and despair. We go from pillar to post. There are too many setbacks.

Moses's day-to-day life seems like a succession of setbacks to him. Sometimes, he gives in: this is when he flies into a rage; his temper explodes, he takes instant action, he thirsts for an absolute solution. When young, he thirsted for human justice: he killed the foreman, parted the fighting Hebrews, protected the Midianite shepherds against marauders. But later, Moses is confronted not merely with individuals but with the obtuseness of human nature itself. And that, in due course, leads him to praise.

First of all, he is confronted with his own obtuseness – in the conversation at the burning bush: 'Go, I am sending you . . . !' – 'Alas, who am I? No, send someone else, I don't know how to speak. I'm no good. Send anyone else you please!' This was his first reaction – an obtuse one and one which he probably regretted bitterly afterwards. And then, there was the massive, heavy obtuseness of his people, their complaints all through the desert, their debauchery, their idolatry.

He dies, baulked of his supreme good, the one thing he has struggled for all his life: entering the Promised Land. And yet, the praise bursts forth, the great passages of *Deuteronomy* resound: 'Then I pleaded with Yahweh; "My Lord Yahweh," I said, "since you have begun to reveal your greatness, the strength of your arm, your inimitable power, to your servant, you whose actions and mighty deeds no one in heaven or on earth can rival . . . please, may I not go across and see that happy country on the other side of the Jordan . . . those happy uplands and the Lebanon?" But God said, "Enough, say no more! Climb to the top of Pisgah, turn your eyes to the west, to the north, to the south and to the east. Take a good look for across this Jordan you will not go!" ' (*Dt* 3: 24–27).

Once again, Moses hopes to see something in close-up, but once again he is only allowed to see it from a distance – the Promised Land – after all the hardships of leading his people to it; it is like his sight of God when under the shadow of his hand, in the cleft in the rock.

'There, on the top of Nebo, died Moses, the servant of Yahweh, on the soil of Moab – with the kiss of God' (*Dt* 34:5–7, trans. Neher). 'Moses was a hundred and twenty years old when he died, his eye undimmed, his vigour unimpaired.'

And so this inextricable mixture of failure and adoration, of good grain and tares, of adoration and intercession for sin, leads Moses to praise, to the *Te Deums* of joy, acclamation and deliverance, which studded his life:

> Yah is my strength and my song,
> to him I owe my deliverance.
> He is my God and I praise him,
> my forefather's God and I extol him.   (*Ex* 15:2)

If Moses sings jubilantly after crossing the Red Sea, he sings even more jubilantly at the end of his life (*Dt* 32:1–2, 4–5):

> Listen, O heavens, while I speak!
> Hear, earth, the words that I shall say!
> May my teaching fall like the rain,
> may my word drop down like the dew!
> For I shall proclaim the name of Yahweh.
> Oh, tell the greatness of our God!
> He is the Rock, his work is perfect.

This is praise: praise wrung from every moment of his life (*Dt* 32:4–5):

> A faithful God, without unfairness,
> He is Rectitude and Righteousness.
> Those whom he had begotten without blemish
> have now become corrupt.

Praise bursts from his intercession, embracing the entire history of his people, of 'this generation deceitful and perverse' yet ever guarded, protected and loved by God (*Dt* 32: 6–12):

> Is this the return you make to Yahweh?
> O foolish people, destitute of wisdom . . .
> Think back on the days of old . . .
> Ask your father, let him teach you . . .
> When the Most High gave the nations their heritage . . .
> But Yahweh's portion was his people,
> Jacob was his upland heritage.

In the country of the steppe he adopts him,
in the horrible solitude of the wilds.
He protects him, rears him, guards him
as the pupil of his eye;
like an eagle watching its nest,
hovering over its young,
he spreads out his wings to hold him,
he supports him on his pinions.
Yahweh alone is his guide.

Moses's whole life explodes in this ultimate certainty.
Though dying within a few yards of the Promised Land, he
never doubts the promise of his God. He is sure that nothing
can impair God's indeflectable fidelity or his immeasurable
love

DAVID

The Miserere

'Let me see your face,' said Moses to the God who was his friend. But this was impossible, even for Moses: 'You cannot see my face, for man cannot see me and live' (*Ex* 33:18–20). Time went by – two or three hundred years – Israel went on seeking the face of its God. And discovered that only upright hearts may contemplate God's countenance, because God is holy and righteous and you have to be like him to see him.

And now, among the many heroes produced by the Israelite nation, comes David. He sings in honour of his Lord, he wants to build him a temple, he cannot bear living in a cedarwood palace himself while the Ark of God is still under canvas. But God doesn't want a temple built by anyone just yet. God, instead, will build the dynasty and sovereignty of David, and these are to last forever. David gives thanks for this: 'Yes, Lord, you are God indeed, your words are true and you have made this fair promise to your servant' (2 *S* 7:28).

Now, in this same David, so gifted and so high-minded, in this young man who stood up to Goliath the giant and was willing to pardon Saul when persecuted by him, in David a very abyss of sin is about to open. It needed a very great man to sin so excessively; mediocre people only have mediocre sins. Moses took his people's sin on himself; David has to carry his own, and all alone.

In a psalm which I should like to think was by David, a verse reads: 'Abyss reverberates to abyss at the crash of your cataracts, and all your billows and breakers go rolling over me' (*Ps* 42:7). The human soul, St. Augustine says in his *Confessions,* is an abyss and, when we speak to a human soul about things divine, we cause the abyssal cataracts of God to pour down into the abyss of the soul. But the human soul can also become an abyss of sin! God plunges into it just the same, on one condition however: that the soul is humbly aware of its own wretchedness.

Physicists of olden days used to say that nature abhors a vacuum. God too, when he sees a soul truly empty of self, rushes to refill it. And this is the lesson for us today, as for St. Augustine long ago, to be found in the school of David and the *Psalms*. Stalin's daughter Svetlana Alliluyeva experienced this to be so and testified impressively to that effect. Svetlana grew up in the very heart of the Kremlin, surrounded by the strictest atheism that ever could be. What woman could be more sensitive to the stresses of that inhumane system, of her own mother having been driven to suicide, and of herself being Stalin's daughter? At the age of thirty-five, she too began to wonder whether suicide wasn't the solution for her. She met Andrei Siniavsky, himself a Christian convert. He introduced her to the Psalms. From that moment, she wrote, 'my life was enriched from an inexhaustible spring, strong as a sun':

'I used to try and put my feelings into words, the better to understand them. Eventually, I found the words in the Psalms of David.

'David sings with heart wide open, with heart beating as though about to burst. He is almost stunned by life, yet in life he sees God. He asks God to come to his help when he feels, from time to time, that he is going wrong; he tells God about his weaknesses, tries to find out where he has been at fault, blames himself for his mistakes, then says that he is less than nothing, one mere atom in the universe: but an atom all the same, and hence thanks God for the universe around him and for the light in his own soul.

'Never have I found words so potent as those of the Psalms. Their burning poetry purges, restores courage, lets you see clearly into yourself, see where you have gone wrong and how to begin again. The Psalms are a great beacon of love and truth.'

What is the secret of the potency of the Psalms? In the language in which God teaches us to address him, there are only two paths (and Jesus says much the same): 'There are two ways. Not three or four or as many as you fancy,' writes André Chouraqui, a great authority on the Psalms. 'It is made clear: the world is divided into *two*. A choice has to be made . . . The way of Darkness and the way of Light between them cover all reality.' Note that modern calculating machines are based on a similarly simple principle: either the current flows or does not flow: there are only two figures – one and zero. Indefinitely repeated, these are enough for the most astronomical calculation you care to make.

In the Psalms, there is the way of the Prince of Darkness. In them, Chouraqui points out, there are one hundred and twelve nouns, names, titles and qualities applied to the Evil One, the Oppressor, the Architect of Negation – the one whom Jesus was to call the 'Raka'. And then there is the way of the Righteous One, the Sedeq, the Blameless One. He is the Architect of the Positive, and he too has some hundred synonyms and epithets: Humble, Poor, Faithful, Godfearing.

You can divide the Psalms along a different line of cleavage if you prefer, again on the binary principle: the Psalms can be divided into Adoration and Poverty. Adoration is expressed and summed up in the one word: *Alleluia!* And poverty (*anawah*) is what is reached 'through experience of distress and human failure', to use A. Gelin's definition. All human life, all human prayer, passes between the twin polarities of adoration and poverty: 'Bless the Lord, O my soul, and my innermost being, his Holy Name!' (103:1) – this is adoration. 'Sing joyfully to the Lord, earth entire, burst into song and music . . . Let the sea and its contents thunder, the world and its whole population, let the ocean-currents clap their hands, the mountains shout for joy all together, at the Lord's approach' (98:4, 7–9). – Rejoicing because the Otherness of God is always and infinitely beyond our powers to express: 'Try as you may, you will never manage to say all.'

The other experience, inseparable from the first, is poverty, poverty compounded with vehemence. Gide called the psalmists 'people who talked to God as man to man.' They don't mince their words with God. They talk to him straight, like Jeremiah: 'You have seduced me, you have overpowered me. Alas that ever I was born!' (*Jr* 20:7, 14). And in the psalms of poverty, misery and suffering – and how very great they are! – we pour out all our own consciousness of misery and sin. 'O Yahweh, my God, my Saviour, day and night I cry to you. May my prayer reach your presence, listen to my cry for help . . . For my soul is full of troubles . . . You have plunged me into the lowest Pit, into the regions deep and dark,' – abyss calls to abyss – 'I am half-blind. Bereft by you of friends and colleagues, my only companion is the Dark' (*Ps* 88).

And here is the poor man. He pleads, and 'the Lord hears him and saves him from all his oppressors,' and even when the poor man protests, he ends by saying, 'Depend on Yahweh and stay calm.' If he wasn't poor, he wouldn't say that, but because he is poor, he knows that God will come to him. 'Enough of anger, leave your rage, settle your hope on Yahweh, keep his way' (*Ps* 37:8, 34). 'Be a faithful shepherd!' The soul relaxes, reassured and at peace.

The bond, culminating in the *Magnificat,* between God's holiness and man's humility, is already seen by Isaiah in his inaugural vision. He sees the angels of God shouting, "Holy, holy, holy is Yahweh. His glory fills the entire earth!" The foundations of the threshold shook at the voice of the one who shouted, and the Temple filled with smoke' – adoration, the vision of divine holiness and majesty – 'and I said, "Alas for me! I am lost, for I am a man of unclean lips and I live among a people of unclean lips" '(*Is* 6:2–5). He is aware of his poverty.

With these two qualities of adoration and poverty firmly in our minds, we now turn to that greatest of all the psalms ascribed to David: the *Miserere.* Even though David can hardly himself have been its author, but more probably some pupil of the Prophet Ezekiel, the author – whoever he was – has exactly explained what David once felt and what we all still feel. David had been carried away by sin. But David, with his true love for God and for God's honour, had a vivid sense of his own frailty – yes, David, monarch though he was. To Nathan who reproached him for his offence, he immediately admitted: 'I have sinned before the Lord' (2 S 12–13). Psalm 51 is the plea of someone who is a sinner and a good man at the same time.

The doctrine of true conversion is summed up in these words: 'Have mercy, pity, my God, pity, O Lord!' Merely by saying this, we have left the zone of remorse and regret and entered the zone of repentance. 'Have pity, my God!' Remorse is still only the feeling of shame caused by the awareness of having done wrong. Remorse is orientated towards the past, it is tied up with self, with my action, my pride perhaps, my hopelessness, Judas sees no opening: despair, pure remorse, regret; he stays orientated towards a past which nothing can now alter. It's all over; whatever you do, what has gone will not return.

Repentance, in contrast, means saying like David, 'Have pity, my God!' Repentance is positive hope in someone else: St. Peter's tears. 'Have pity on me, O God, in your kindness, in your great mercy blot out my offences.' And then, the immediate request for purification: 'Wash me of my guilt,' this is hopeful already: 'Purify me from my sin. I am only too aware of my offences; I have my sin constantly in mind.' Yes, David had been an adulterer and his adultery had led him on to murder; even so, his sense of God was deep enough for him to be able to avow to his Lord: 'I have sinned against none other than you, having done what you regard as wrong' (*Ps* 51:1–4).

His sin does not reside in graduated homicide, even less in degrees of sexual activity, but primarily in having ruptured his personal relationship with God: true, even if I have committed murder! There is no sin and can be no repentance except in relation to God recognised as loving, as waiting for something from me, as inviting me to love him in return. 'Adam, where are you?' That was what God said after Adam had sinned. And we, for our part, reply, 'I heard your footsteps. I was afraid. I hid' (*Gn* 3:10). The rupturing of a personal relationship with God – I hide from God. I make a free act of choice: to refuse God when he approaches. Human circumstances clothe and colour the sin, but it is still, primarily, a rejection of God.

Isaiah puts this well in the opening verses of his book: 'Listen, you heavens: earth, attend: for Yahweh is speaking! "I raised sons, I brought them up, but they have rebelled against me." ' The revolt is sin. The text develops the antithesis between the two words, revolt and knowledge. 'The ox knows its owner, and the ass its master's crib. Israel knows nothing, my people understand nothing.' Knowledge is this quasi-marital intimacy in which both parties know each other through and through: 'O sinful nation, they have abandoned me, they have turned their backs on me!' (*Is* 1:24). Thus, revolt against God runs counter to knowledge of God. Contrariwise, when Hosea speaks of coming back to God – 'I shall betroth you to myself in faithfulness' – as opposed to revolt – 'and you will know Yahweh' (*Ho* 2:22) – he always uses the word knowledge.

The obscuring of God's light if we persist in sin is a serious matter: sin hardens, forms a sort of crust over our skin, an outer shell of dirt. You remember what Jeremiah says: 'Can the Ethiopian change his skin? Can the leopard change its spots? And you, can you do what is right, you so accustomed to do wrong?' (*Jr* 13:23). But the poor man, the humble one, is precisely he who does know that he can always change his course, turn round, retrace his steps, and have a change of heart: two things that go together. Christians have always held on to this as a sure hope. You recall Pascal, in the *Mystery of Jesus*, where Christ says to him: 'If you knew your sins, you would lose heart.' – 'Then I shall lose heart, Lord.' – 'No, because I who tell you this intend to cure you of them, and what I am telling you is the sign that I intend to cure you.'

Thus, in the self-same glance, David discovers God and discovers his own wickedness. 'Have pity on me, O God, in your kindness, blot out my offences, wash me of my guilt, for I am only too aware of my offences, having sinned against none other than you, having done what you regard as wrong.' In God's mercy, David discovers his own abjection, the extreme opposite, but nonetheless full of hope, thanks to the grand affirmation in another psalm: 'By your light, we shall see the light.'

Once more, the call to inner renewal rings out: 'Let me hear songs of joy and gladness, let the bones that you have crushed rejoice' (51:8). David comes out of his self-isolating silence, the silence of someone unwilling to avow his fault. 'Silence was wasting my bones away' (32:3).

Dear St. Francis of Sales, who had some pretty odd ideas about natural history but was a good hand at a parable, says that when a wolf wants to catch a sheep, if it attacks the sheep by its trotters, the sheep baas, the shepherd comes and chases the wolf away; next time, the cunning wolf catches the sheep by the throat, the sheep can't make a sound and it carries it off: no problem. There you have it. 'Silence wastes my bones away' when I cannot bring myself to admit my fault, but is transformed into wondrous praise once I return to my allegiance: 'For you, O God, silence is praise' (as they used to translate *Ps* 65:1).

And now, David is reorientated for thanksgiving: 'Turn your face away from my sins and blot out all the wrongs that I have done.' And he then says something very extraordinary: 'O God, create me a pure heart!'

This verb 'to create' used here is only used in the Bible when speaking of God. God is the only subject of this verb 'to create', never man. Which means that the 're-creation' implored by David, cannot be a human operation, nor the fruit of sacrifices, nor the result of atonement. The changing of the heart is an operation which only the God of *Genesis*, the Creator of heaven and earth, can perform.

'Do not banish me ... do not deprive me of your Holy Spirit. O Lord, inspire my lips . . . Should you be pleased by a sacrifice, I would offer one . . . But the best sacrifice of all is a contrite spirit. A heart contrite and crushed, spurn not, O God!' (*Ps* 51:10–17).

Here we ought to pause for a moment. In Israel, there were all sorts of expiatory sacrifices for every kind of fault, but not for adultery and not for murder. For these, the punishment prescribed for the guilty party was death, and nothing else. But what legal tribunal could pass sentence on a king, a theocratic king at that, who was simultaneously chief magistrate and the Lord's Anointed? Unthinkable that he should be stoned or lynched. David was trapped in an insoluble dilemma: he had an obligation to atone for his crime, but no means by which he could do so. There were, of course, the scourges predicted by Nathan, but these would not have been endured by David in person; he would only have to endure them indirectly, in his capacity of father and husband. David aspired to make personal reparation, but could not expiate his crime by dying, since no court had a mandate to pass judgment on him.

At this point, David intuitively discovers an extraordinary and hitherto unknown route: 'Should you be pleased by a sacrifice? A heart contrite and crushed, spurn not, O God!' The inward offering will have to take the place of atonement by sacrifice. Not enough, of course, to have a fleeting moment of contrition – a moment of shame is soon over, as my lady-neighbour in Marseilles used to say – but the best sacrifice of all, accepted by God, is unquestionably hearty contrition accompanied by humility and frank avowal.

Five hundred years later, an analogous situation, – though the external circumstances are entirely different – produces the same dilemma. Zedekiah, David's last successor on the throne, has been captured, taken into captivity, put in chains and blinded. The craftsmen, the young people, have all been deported and, among the useful Israelites, Ananiah, Azariah and Mishael. These three young martyrs, out of all the rest, refuse to worship Nebuchadnezzar's gigantic statue.

They are thrown into the furnace, ostensibly for having refused to obey the king, but in fact, in the sight of God, because of the sins of Israel. They too can say, 'We have sinned against none other than you.' True, they have refused to worship idols, but in solidarity with their nation they bear the shame of all. 'For in truth and justice, you have treated us like this because of our sins. Yes, we have sinned, committed a crime by deserting you. Yes, we have gravely sinned. We have not listened to your commandments, we have not observed them, we have not done what we were told to do for our own good . . . Oh, do not abandon us forever . . . do not repudiate your covenant, do not withdraw your favour from us, for the love of Abraham your friend,' – Abraham's first title – 'of Isaac, . . . of Israel. See, we are humiliated by everyone on earth today, because of our sins' (*Dn* 3:28–37).

Now, Mishael, Ananiah and Azariah, just like David, are quite unable to offer the atoning sacrifices. They are deportees, there is no temple where they are, there is no priest. 'In these days, we have no leader, no prophet, no prince, no holocaust, no sacrifice, no oblation, no incense, no place where we can make offerings to you and win your favour.'

They too, faced with death, find themselves in an insoluble dilemma as regards God. They wish to atone for the whole people, but their wish cannot be fulfilled: they cannot offer the atoning sacrifices. Only the divine solution remains, the same as David's; Azariah has the same thought as David and expresses it in the same words: 'But may the contrite soul, the humbled spirit, be acceptable to you.' Azariah explains: 'As holocausts of rams and bullocks, as thousands of fat lambs, such let our sacrifice be to you today, and may it please you that we follow you wholeheartedly, since those who hope in you are never disappointed' (*Dn* 3:38–40).

'A heart contrite and crushed, spurn not, O God!' For Azariah, as for David, the desire to atone according to the regulations cannot be fulfilled. He therefore offers his broken soul, his humbled spirit; he repeats the prayer in the psalm; and the humility of his heart compensates for the thousands of fat sheep. He knows that this confidence will not be disappointed, for he goes on to add, which David could not, the gift of the lives of all three: 'Such let our sacrifice be to you today'; yes, a contrite heart and their presence in the furnace.

Now, this concerns us too. In the sacrifice which we offer during the Eucharist, Christ is not offered on his own – how hard this is to grasp! – but the whole Body of Christ, the whole Mystical Body, offered to become, in Christ, 'a living sacrifice to the praise of God's glory.'

Now, how is this to be expressed, not in this or that prayer, but in *each* Eucharist? How are we to express this gift of ourselves, this personal participation by each of us in the sacrifice? (The word participation is too weak, but what else can we say?) Well, we shall repeat, word for word, the prayer of Azariah! *'In spiritu humilitatis et in animo contrito suscipiamur Domine a te'* . . . And, saying over the words of Azariah, we say over the very words of David, even if in translation it is sometimes hard to identify them as such. At each Eucharist, we stand with Azariah in the furnace, with David in his sin.

It is, I suppose, easier to say, 'Humble and poor, we plead with you, O Lord' or something of that sort. But the fact is that it would be better to repeat Azariah's very words: 'May a contrite soul, a humbled spirit, be acceptable to you; such be our sacrifice to you today and may we truly please you!'

This is how we enter the line of these great men, this is how we participate in Christ's action; today, we too plead with him to give us a heart contrite, humbled, crushed, broken – call it what you will – the inward sacrifice of the heart.

This is the heritage bequeathed to us by David: beyond our faults, the true sacrifice is when a man offers himself entirely to God, bringing nothing to him but his wretchedness and the hope of a total renewal in Him. 'Create me a pure heart . . . A heart contrite and crushed, spurn not, O God.' There is certainty here: nothing, no sin however murderous it be can separate the repentant heart from God.

The paschal lamb had to be a lamb without spot, without blemish, perfect; and yet God, if we have a repentant heart, accepts our rottenness; and probably, until we have discovered our own rottenness, we cannot have a truly contrite heart. The saints, for their part, discovered the rottenness without having sinned too much first; for us, it may be that we shall have to fall very low. And possibly the matter with some of us is that we haven't fallen sufficiently low to plead, 'Create me a pure heart!' Better not take too much of a chance, perhaps!

This prayer, humbly repeated at each Eucharist as a means, having offered the bread and wine, of showing our own participation, our own willingness to share in the sacrifice, will bring us face to face with the cruellest aspects of modern life. When we consider the horrors of modern life, war, famine and drought – even when we contemplate all this from a distance – our sleepy consciences will be touched. What should we do? Condemn? that's easily done – condemn. Condemn the woman who has an abortion? Condone? Yes, that is easy too. But neither solution is satisfactory. There is no clean choice. Either way, we shall have guilt on our hands, or indeed, as Péguy would say, we shall have no hands. Nor is the lesser of two evils something good.

Class-war, subversion, insurrection, torture, the taking of
hostages, the death penalty, the whole apparatus of violence
hems us in on all sides, whether we take part in it or not. We
too know the insoluble dilemma of David and Azariah.

Death in the soul for us, if we affirm the law of perfection
given us by Christ – without being sure of our deeper motives
when we wax indignant. Death in the soul for us, if we close
our eyes to tragic situations, while knowing that these by ex-
tension can lead to a general degradation of society. Thus,
whether we condone or condemn, we are still sinners. A
medical friend of mine, Dr. Charles Nodet, writes: 'The
human condition requires us to accept this contradiction
serenely and constantly adjust ourselves to it. Our destiny lies
in conflict, and this is never resolved, if we accept it
clear-headedly, not with approval, not with disgust, loaded as
it is with our own wretchedness.'

One prayer, the Hail Mary, is highly apposite here. After
the angelic salutation and the words of Elizabeth ('Blessed art
thou among women') comes like the roar of ocean the prayer
of humanity entire: 'Holy Mary, Mother of God, pray for us
poor sinners.'

Let us therefore ask Christ's Mother for the grace to be
made aware of our sinfulness. Not remorse for it, but repentance and inward sacrifice. 'To want the good is within my
scope, but not to do it. I do not do the good which I wish. I do
the evil, which I hate. Who will deliver me from this living
death? Thanks be to God, through Jesus Christ our Lord' (*Rm*
7:18–19, 24–25).

THE ANAWIM

The prayer of the poor and lowly

After Abraham, the man of faith who set out relying exclusively on the Word of God; after Moses, the man of intercession who shaped a nation; after the prayer of David the penitent: we now look at the host of lowly, poor, unimportant, anonymous people with enough on their plates already in merely earning a living, without undertaking great enterprises. People who, in the words of the Psalm, say 'Lord, my heart is not haughty, I do not meddle with matters too lofty for me' (131:1). These are the lowly people of the world, the silent people, the silent keepers of the faith, people whose prayers do not appear in our spiritual manuals – nonetheless people by whom, century after century, the faith is kept alive.

Apparently – and here I don't want to offend any sympathisers with the Reformation – apparently, according to historians, one or two hundred years after Luther's death, many Lutheran pastors were no longer quite convinced of the divinity of Christ. – Was he truly God? Thanks to their studies, they had come to doubt it. But the people in the pews, with their simple love of God, with their psalm-singing and Bach chorales in church of a Sunday, and their simple, uncritical reading of the Scriptures, were the ones through whom faith in Jesus Christ was kept alive. They were what we should today call 'the faceless ones', nonplussed by the subtle and learned controversies carried on over their heads. Not that this means that the learned are automatically excluded from the ranks of the poor and lowly. No one is shut out, learned men included, provided that, however learned they may be, they stay open-minded, docile, *teachable*.

Let us try and characterise the silent prayer of the poor and lowly, of the majority at prayer even when unaware of praying.

What is being poor, for a start? It means being dependent on someone else. Being poor and sick means being dependent on the doctor, on the nurse in the hospital, on social security and what not. Being cold means that someone else has to give you clothes. You are without resources. Being poor means being dependent on someone else and receiving help from someone else – to a greater or lesser extent, but basically that.

But then, if being poor means receiving from and depending on someone else, it follows that we cannot make ourselves poor: to want to make oneself poor is a contradiction in terms. One cannot 'make one's way' and at the same time 'receive from someone else'. Either I make my way, or I receive. If being poor means receiving from and being dependent on someone else, I cannot in fact make myself poor. But spiritual poverty itself is always 'received'. I can, of course, always divest myself of worldly things, I can throw my clothes away, give my possessions to others and so forth. But I am talking of something deeper. One receives spiritual poverty by looking and listening. By this, I do not mean by sitting back and doing nothing, but by really looking and by really listening. Looking and listening are two activities which inevitably take us out of ourselves. When I look, I come out of myself; when I listen, I come out of myself. Things catch my eye, my ear, which take them in. Forthwith, I am no longer shut in on myself. But listening to and looking at what? At whom? Well, at Jesus, who describes himself – this translation seems the best – as 'modest and humble of heart' (*Mt* 11:29). Note that, when Jesus says this, it comes immediately after his vivid act of thanksgiving to the Father, 'who reveals himself to mere children' and 'hides himself from the learned and the clever' (*Mt* 11:25). Gentleness is the result and outward sign of inner modesty: Jesus is gentle and humble of heart because he is modest. He, the Word, is the very opposite of the 'Stand aside! Make way for me!' sort.

To be poor, we have to observe God's behaviour, God's mentality and actions, so to speak. And this is exactly what the poor and humble seek, find and get in the Bible. When

Jesus says, 'Learn from me', he means listen and then do the same. He, being modest and humble of heart, will make us modest and humble of heart. As we have already seen, God forgives anyone and anything: David was an adulterer and murderer, the tax-collector in the parable was a traitor and extortioner. God does not pick and choose: he takes the job-lot, even if some of it isn't as fresh as it might be. But there is one thing that God cannot tolerate, one thing that blocks him off – and since there are no psycho-analysts for him to consult, blocked off he stays! God is blocked by one thing: if we think of ourselves as someone, if we take ourself for more than we are, he can do nothing. The great thing about Southern Europeans is that, although they often tend to take things dramatically – and this is often a literary convention – they do not take themselves seriously at all; and this is why God loves them. But when we take ourselves for someone, take ourselves seriously, it is so silly that God doesn't know what to do. Then, as the Bible tells us, he either 'flies into a rage', or sends his Son, as in the parable of the murderous vine-dressers (*Mt* 21:33).

Psalm 95, sung morning after morning by Church and Synagogue alike, daily invites us to remember that praying must be done humbly. 'Let us worship, bowing low, let us kneel to Yahweh our Maker, for he is our God. Do not be obstinate today.' But if people won't listen, the Lord reacts with loathing and anger: 'I think these are a fickle-hearted people. Never are they to enter that restful place of mine!' And see too, in *Deuteronomy*, that long passage where the Lord instructs us not to become 'proud of heart' (8:11–17).

How does God set about it? What are his methods for trying to teach us to be poor, poor in heart? God acts on two levels simultaneously. First, he acts through the minority, and of the minority only preserves 'a remnant'. And secondly, he acts on the small potentialities, through the penury, of each individual. The doctrine of the 'little remnant' is a law, a divine constant, a central message, which God teaches us throughout the Scriptures. The law has two aspects: one of them is catastrophic – of Israel only a little remnant, a minute bud,

one shoot, will survive; but the other aspect is rich in promise:
a remnant will escape. God always insists on this: the
catastrophic or apparently catastrophic sense, the fact that
few will survive, is basic but never unqualified. Hence, Isaiah
has this extraordinary sentence: 'Israel your people may be
like the sand on the seashore, but only a remnant will return.
A destruction has been decreed which will make justice
overflow' (*Is* 10:22) and yet God has given Isaiah's son the
symbolic name, the hopeful name: 'A remnant will return'
(7:3).

Only 'two little bones and a bit of an ear' will be rescued
from the lion – not much. The lion will have gobbled up the
rest. But there is still this little bit of ear left; and with this,
God will do amazing things (*Am* 3:12), as he will with the two
olives right at the top of the tree. Of the whole olive-tree there
are only two miserable little olives left! But starting from
these, everything will begin again (*Is* 17:6). Of the stock of the
tree, nine-tenths have been cut away (*Is* 6:13) but – here is the
hopeful aspect – there is always something left. And that little
remaining will put out new roots, new fruits; the little remaining will in its turn become as strong as a lion: the sacrificial
lamb described in the *Book of Revelation*.

This then, is the first thing that God always makes us
realise. The younger is chosen in preference to the elder: Abel
in preference to Cain, Isaac to Ishmael, Jacob to Esau, Rachel
to Leah, Joseph and David to all their brothers. He who had
no expectations, who was the last, who had been left with the
sheep by his father, was the one to be chosen by God to save
his entire people. This primary law is stated by St. Paul, and
few have known the Scriptures better than he: 'To shame
what is strong, God chose what is by human reckoning weak;
those whom the world thinks common and contemptible are
the ones whom God has chosen – those who are nothing at all,
to show up those who are everything; so that the human race
will have nothing to boast about to God' (1 *Co* 1:27–29).

Israel is well aware of having been chosen. Forthwith,
Moses puts the nation on its guard: 'If Yahweh has set his
heart on you and chosen you, this is not because you are the
most numerous of all peoples – for you are in fact the least

numerous of all peoples – but because he loves you' (*Dt* 7:7–8). This is the divine constant: Operation 'Gideon'. Gideon had too many soldiers to fight the battle in Yahweh's name. God had therefore to devise all sorts of expedients to whittle the number down: finally there was scarcely a handful left and these were the ones who were committed to battle, for at this point it had become impossible to harbour any further illusions: God saves, and none other. Yahweh said to Gideon, 'There are too many (!) people with you, for me to put your enemies into your power. Israel might claim the credit for themselves at my expense, they might say, "My own hand has rescued me!" ' (*Jg* 7:2). So there we have the first law: the law of small numbers, little remnants, so that God can show his power for what it is.

Furthermore, and second law: the law of very penurious little remnants. In Psalm 119, God tells us why he makes us poor. There are three very illuminating verses: 'Before I was afflicted, I went astray, but now I keep your word.' – 'It has done me good to have to suffer, so that I could learn your statutes.' – 'I know, Yahweh, that you are just, that you made me suffer in the cause of truth' (*Ps* 119:67, 71, 75). This is how we ought to pray. Once we have been impoverished by God, that is the moment when anything can be done. 'Just in your judgments, Yahweh, you have made me suffer.' These three verses are the peak of spiritual poverty, and this itself constitutes the backbone of the entire Old and New Testaments.

In olden days, the Latin word used to express these qualities ('poor', 'humble', 'gentle') was *mansuetus, mansuetudo,* which comes from the word *mansuesco,* meaning literally 'to become used to the hand' of someone, as a horse becomes used to the hand of its rider. The poor man is the man in God's hand, whom God has succeeded in taming, who is no longer afraid, who no longer tries to escape, who rests in God's hand.

The connexion between God's people and the poor and lowly is explained to us in the Bible. But by whom? By a prophet – yes, of course! By Isaiah? By Ezekiel? By one of those so-called 'Major' prophets'? Well, they do indeed talk about it, but the message is primarily one of a 'minor' prophet, more

minor even than Hosea, of a very minor prophet indeed whom
we do not often read. This prophet is even more minor than
Amos, more minor than Hosea, more minor than Joel. You
can see that he has to be very minor indeed for us not to be
able to think of his name: Zephaniah, a very, very minor
prophet! They are called minor because they didn't write
much. Not because they carried less weight than the major
ones, but because they didn't make so much work at the
printers. And Zephaniah it was, in about 640 BC, who first
identified the nation of the future, the messianic nation, the
people of God – the people whom we want to be – as the
nation of the poor. 'When that day comes, you need feel no
more shame for the misdeeds which you have committed
against me, for I shall remove your proud boasters from your
midst' – this is what God intends to do, so that the people may
become his once more – 'and you will cease to strut on my
holy mountain. In your midst, I shall leave a humble and lowly people, and those who are left in Israel will seek refuge in
the Name of Yahweh' (*Zp* 3:11–13).

This is the first time that the idea of the remnant of Israel is
linked to that of a poor, humble, little people. Because Israel
was dominated by Assyria, because it was in a state of
national humiliation, the flowering of a new people became
possible. What God waits for, so that he can intervene to exert
his power and save his people – 'they will be able to graze and
rest with no one to disturb them' – is a humble people with
modest resources, not necessarily people with no money, but a
humble people with limited possibilities.

There are several stages for this humble people to go
through, before becoming 'the little remnant' that Yahweh
has in mind.

First stage: humility alone makes the prophets, those who
speak in God's name; humility alone makes the poor, the
anawim. We have to know this word, because it is really un-
translatable. Moses, as we already know, was 'the humblest of
all', a man in whom modesty was absolute. The other
prophets weren't as modest as Moses, who was 'the humblest
man who ever walked on earth' and 'there has never been such
a prophet in Israel as Moses' (*Dt* 34:10); and consequently

their personalities never developed quite as fully as his. Modesty means accepting oneself for what one is, and by so doing a man can make the most of himself. The man whose personality is most perfectly developed thus achieves the highest degree of prophetic power. Humility and modesty transform the poor man into the man of God. Without these qualities, we should just go on being poor. The Bible uses a great many words to designate 'the poor man': the indigent, thin, weak, the hungry beggar, the humiliated man – all Hebrew terms denoting 'the poor man', the sufferer, the afflicted, the man brought low: but if there is no humility, which is what makes the *anawim* what they are, the whole exercise is useless, as St. Paul says when writing about charity.

This was what Isaiah was also saying: 'Thus speaks the Most High: I live in the holy heights, but I also live with the contrite and humble heart. The earth is my footstool, nonetheless my eyes are drawn to the man of humbled and contrite heart' (*Is* 57:15; 66:1–2).

St. Augustine uses these words of Isaiah when commenting on the beatitude in the Sermon on the Mount. 'Who are the poor in spirit?' and he answers. 'The humble, who confess their sins, who do not pride themselves on their merits or their righteousness. Who are the poor in spirit? Those who praise God when they do right, but hold themselves to blame when they do wrong.' He then adapts Isaiah (66:2): 'On whom shall my spirit rest,' says the prophet, 'if not on the humble man, the man of peace, who trembles at my word?'

In a word, on these 'anawim' who are mentioned so often in the Bible. And of them we can say that they abound in nothing so much as in their poverty. Their only wealth lies in having nothing; they are men tried and matured by suffering, who from it have learnt the truest humility of all: abandonment to God. In the midst of their trials, they know that God is near. This is the first stage: a humility transforming a poor man into a man of God, into a devoted man, as Scripture calls it.

Second stage: out of these poor men, these anawim, humility fashions the mystical nucleus of the nation. They comprise the little, saving remnant, they are the leaven in the dough, and hence, despite themselves, through no intention of theirs, they find themselves in conflict with the majority. Because of having entered the way of God, they find themselves, already with more than enough problems of their own, having to face up to people who refuse to listen, to people of tepid devotion who say, 'My word, how you do go on!' – to people only interested in power, money, culture, those who put politics first.

The confrontation is dramatically sketched in Psalms 9–10: 'God remembers, he does not forget the cry of the afflicted – of the anawim.' But, confronting the afflicted, are the arrogant. 'Yahweh, why do you keep so distant? Why do you hide, now that the times are bad? The wicked man is always brewing harm for others, panting to carry out schemes which he has laid. The wicked man is contemptuous of Yahweh: "The Lofty One, if offended, will not seek vengeance. God will not interfere with my plans." – O Exalted One, your laws are alien to him, it is his very nature to sniff at them. "Nothing can shift me," he sincerely believes, "happy forever and ever immune to misfortune". He spends his time in cursing, lying and browbeating.'

The poor man is trapped in the arrogant man's net, and the wicked man, not being able to kill God, kills the poor man instead.

This first factor (the humility characterising the poor man) and this second factor (the more or less mocking and hostile environment of the anawim) group them together. Is this for a bit of comfort? Be that as it may! Because of these factors, anawim love other anawim, they have a sense of community and, as André Gelin remarks, this sense of community is worth some emphasis: the anawim love to meet in groups. 'I shall give thanks to Yahweh with all my heart in the council of the upright and in the assembly' (*Ps* 111). For this reason, it is 'very good and pleasant when brothers live in harmony'. The poor have to congregate in groups, whether organised ones or not, and indeed we see that in countries still remaining poor, a brotherly kind of life, social life with long conversations, plays a much greater part than in rich countries like our own. Look at Brazil, Africa, or anywhere in the Third World. 'How very good and pleasant it is for brothers to live in harmony, fine as

oil on the head, running down the beard, down Aaron's
beard!' St. Augustine said that the words of this psalm (133)
had given birth to the monasteries.

Jesus was surrounded by anawim, by a whole populace of
the poor and lowly. For him, they were an occasion for
thanksgiving to the Father: 'I bless you, Father, for everything
that you have revealed to these little ones,' and they too will
teach us how to pray. There is no need to rack our brains
over the method. All we have to do is to read the Bible and
consider Zechariah and Elizabeth, Simeon and Anna, John
the Baptist, the shepherds, the Samaritan woman and all the
other people waiting 'for the consolation of Israel'. Their
poverty fitted them for receiving the gift of God – which in fact
they were expecting, without knowing quite what it would be:
'If you only knew what God is offering you.' All of them were
to some extent under-privileged and humiliated people.
Elizabeth and Zechariah were righteous in the sight of God,
irreproachable indeed, but it was a great humiliation in those
days for a woman, and a great deprivation for a man, to have
no children. She was sterile and he was very old. Simeon and
Anna, two old folk, she a widow and on her own. The
shepherds: humble people putting their faith in what the
angels told them. The Samaritan woman, very sinful, yet
obscurely waiting for the Messiah to come and sort everything
out.

All these teach us how to pray. Though all cobbled up from
the Old Testament – I may venture to say – they set the Old
Testament blossoming into the New. With them, praying isn't
inventing something new, but putting new life into something
old. If you read the *Benedictus* carefully (*Lk* 1:67–79), you will
find it all there: the Psalms, the Prophets – if you consult the
references in the margin you will find half a dozen different
prophets – *Genesis, Leviticus, Numbers* and so on. All this surges
up again in Zechariah's prayer. The ancient tradition
re-asserts itself in its own words: God visits his people, God's
power to save, the House of David, the Covenant, the oath, old
Abraham: all these are there, as well as the bowels of compassion, the messianic age, the Rising Sun, the darkness, the

shadow of death – all blossoming afresh into a song full of
youth and vitality, since it is all coming true *now,* actually
happening at last, everything being renewed. When we recite
the *Benedictus,* we too can make it ring out fresh and new. And
we should also stand back from time to time to admire it.
What a fine old canticle! How good it is to say: 'Blessed be the
Lord, the God of Israel, he has come at last to ransom his
people!' Nice to stand back, but important to make it our own
song too. No need for other prayer, since this song celebrates
the eternal today of God.

With the Samaritan woman, we find a host of pitiful people
existing on the margin of society: their prayer springs from
poverty. We are often told not to turn our backs on life. But
these people are absolutely immersed in it. Their prayer certainly springs from life: 'Lord, give me some of that water, so
that I may never get thirsty and never have to come here again
to draw water' (*Jn* 4:1–42). In Western Europe we have large-
ly forgotten what it's like to go to the spring with a pitcher on
our head. But plenty of women in the world still know what it
feels like to do that.

And the quarantined leper, for instance. But this would
take too long. There are too many of them. Enough merely to
open the Gospel and note down the cries and pleas of all those
poor people, nameless people, whose calls for help are all that
we know about them. The unclean leper throwing himself on
the ground and shouting, 'Lord, if you want to, you can cure
me!' The Roman centurion, another unclean person, experiencing the worst deprivation that a mature man can – the
death of his child (*Mt* 8:5–13; *Jn* 4:46–55): 'Lord, my child is
lying at home, paralysed. Come, Lord, before my child dies!'

And the gem, enshrined and repeated for all time in the
liturgy: 'Lord, I am not worthy to have you under my roof.
Just give the word!' (*Mt* 8:8; *Lk* 7:6). These are prayers of
really humble people, prayers wrung out of their direct experience of life.

There are also vocational prayers: 'Master, where do you
live?' (*Jn* 1:38). This is a way in which we could begin to pray:
'Master, where do you live?' You are in my heart, you are in
my brothers, you are here. And all the budding vocations,

prayers welling up in the confusion of departure when Jesus announces that he is leaving for pagan territory: 'Master, I shall follow you wherever you go?' – 'Foxes have holes, birds have nests . . . ' (*Mt* 8:19; *Lk* 9:57–58).

'Lord, let me go and bury my father first.' – 'Follow me, leave the dead to bury their dead' (*Mt* 8:21–22). For each of these prayers, we have Jesus's reply. The reply to our own prayer too – don't we know it!

And the shouts and tears in the storm: 'Save us, Lord, we are going down!' (*Mt* 8:25). 'Master, don't you care? We are going down!' (*Mk* 4:38–40). Note the difference between *Matthew* and *Mark*, depending on how upset we are. When all is going well, when we feel in the pink, we say, 'Save us, Lord, we are going down!' But when we are out of sorts or in a turn, we say, 'Hey! What are you thinking about? Pay attention! Don't you care if we are going down?' Jesus tells us what our proper attitude should be: 'Why are you so frightened? How is it that you have no faith?' (*Mk* 4:40). This puts us in our place, at prayer. Afterwards, we can say, 'Who can this be? Even the wind and sea obey him!' (*Mt* 8:27; *Mk* 4:41; *Lk* 8:25).

And the saving of Peter: here is another nugget of prayer. This is the missionary's prayer, the creed of the Missions: 'Lord, if it is you, tell me to come to you across the water!' This is when we sign on and take the first few steps (*Mt* 14:28–33). But then the wind begins to blow, the water gets rough, there is nothing to stand on, the Order has got the dry-rot – problems all round! Then, 'Lord, save me!' – that's the prayer, the shout of the poor man who has lost his assurance. And the response: 'Man of little faith, why did you doubt?' – 'Truly, you are the Son of God!' This is the way the poor pray, the humble folk who we must become.

From Peter, the answer to his first shout for help evokes a second missionary prayer: 'Lord, we have worked hard all night long and caught nothing, but if you say so, I shall pay out the nets.' And forthwith, at the amazing catch: 'Leave me, Lord, I am a sinful man!' – 'Don't be afraid; from now on, men are what you are going to catch!' (*Lk* 5:4–11).

Then there are all those pitiful, desperate appeals ('Lord,

have pity on me, Son of David!') of the Canaanite woman with her puppy-dogs (*Mt* 15:22). 'Lord, take pity on my son!' cries the father of the epileptic child (*Mt* 17; *Mk* 9; *Lk* 9). The appeal for help from the man who has no friends at all: 'Lord, I have no one to lower me into the pool' (*Jn* 5:7), of the blind men on the road, 'Lord, Son of David, take pity on us!' – 'What do you want me to do for you?' – 'Let us have our sight back! Let me see again!' – 'Go, your faith has saved you' (*Mt* 20; *Mk* 10; *Lk* 18). The apostles ask: 'Lord, increase our faith' (*Lk* 17:5). The lepers all asking at the same time: 'Jesus, Master, take pity on us!' although only one of them, one out of the ten, comes back again publicly to thank God (*Lk* 17:12–19). The man born blind, who doesn't specifically ask for anything but whose cry, whose poverty, Jesus sees and hears: 'Do you believe in the Son of Man?' – 'Tell me who he is, so that I may believe in him!' – 'You are looking at him. He is speaking to you.' – 'Lord, I believe!' then throws himself at his feet.

Such are the prayers of the crowd, of the nameless ones, of people perhaps who only met Christ once, as he happened to be passing. But what about those closer relationships, those deeply-felt prayers of people who knew Christ better? Martha: 'Lord, the man whom you love is sick . . . If you had been here, my brother would not have died' (*Jn* 11:2, 21). These too are prayers, prayers wrung from life, ' . . . but I know that, whatever you ask of God, he will grant you.'

Whenever we say: 'Lord, come to my help, O God; come quickly and help me,' we should also, Martha-like, say the words: 'Yes, Lord, I believe that you are the Christ, the Son of God, the one who was to come into this world.' And Mary quietly re-echoes Martha's words: 'Lord, if you had been here, my brother would not have died.'

Then there were the people who listened to the great discourse on the Bread of Life: 'Lord, give us that bread always!' You can see, everything we need for a prayer is there. 'What are we to do, if we are to do the works that God wants?' – 'This is working for God: you must believe.' – 'Lord, you have the message of eternal life. We believe. And we know that you are the Holy One of God' (*Jn* 6:26–71). 'Lord, teach us to

pray' (*Lk* 11:1). 'Lord, let us see the Father and then we shall
be satisfied' (*Jn* 14:8). 'Lord, you know everything. You know
I love you' (*Jn* 21:17).

Among these anawim stands Mary, the Queen of the humble – for dignity and humility meet in her. All the anawim of
the Old Testament are, as it were, concentrated in her. God
the Father gathered all the waters together, in *Genesis,* and
called them the seas *(maria)*; he gathered all his graces
together and called them Mary *(Maria)* – thus, charmingly,
Grignion de Montfort. In Mary, we hear the prayer, the
aspiration, the very breathing of all the anawim, of all the
poor, of all the humble people who ever lived.

Here again, ancient tradition bursts into a second spring.
Mary is the end, the crown, of all those people who have been
waiting and listening so intently over the centuries: each of the
anawim, each member of the true New Israel, has been
preparing for, has prefigured, Mary. She lived in Nazareth
with Jesus: 'Can anything good come out of Nazareth?' (*Jn*
1:46). It's the same thing all over again. A place with no past
and of no standing – and that's the one that attracts God's
eye. 'Why,' Bérulle asks, 'did the Angel of the Annunciation,
disregarding triumphant Rome, wise Athens, proud Babylon
and even holy Jerusalem, go to that little-known and despised
market-town? – Yes, it is mysterious. But the reason was that
there the Angel found a silence, a void, a call, a woman
modest before God and men who would ponder the meaning
of the Angel's greeting. The Angel intends to raise the Virgin
and the Virgin abases herself, and Bérulle says: 'God hides
her from mortals by the secret of her virginity, he hides her
even better from herself by the weight of her humility.'

And now we must come to a close, with the anawim's finest
prayer, their prayer of prayers, Mary's *Magnificat,* the very
blueprint of prayer – unique. It is a prayer of total self-abnega-
tion, hence all possibilities are open; all is comprised in three
six-line stanzas. First, the joy of a humble heart trembling
before the majesty of God, trembling like those before God in
the *Psalms.* 'His humble maid was not beneath his notice.'
Humble – the very name of the anawim. Jesus, having received so much from Mary, later re-turned this strophe of the

Magnificat: 'I bless you, Father, Lord of heaven and earth, for having hidden these things from the learned and the clever and for revealing them to mere children' (*Mt* 11:25; *Lk* 10:21).

She rejoices at being a servant, she the mother of the Servant, for the Servant is whom she is going to bring into the world. 'Great is the Lord, my soul proclaims; with all my heart I exult in God my Saviour, for his humble maid was not beneath his notice.'

Mary repeats the same prophecy as Elizabeth, for both of them are prophetesses: 'Of all women, you are the most blessed. Why should I be honoured with a visit from the mother of my Lord? Yes, blessed is she who believed . . . ' (*Lk* 1:42–45). Mary repeats it, but re-phrases it in honour of the Almighty: 'Yes, all ages to come will hail me as blessed, for the Almighty has called me to greatness.'

Greatness, great things, the marvellous deeds of God! But here is something greater than the Red Sea, much greater than the Exodus and manna and covenant in the wilderness. All is summed up in the next line: 'Yes, oh yes, holy is his Name!' 'May your Name be held holy!' Jesus said (*Mt* 6:9; *Lk* 11:2), the Divine Name, the Name revealed to Abraham and Moses, is the mountain top from which Mary next surveys the whole human race.

Then begins the song of the Incarnation. Touching on three forms of human greatness, three forms of human conceit which spoil all (pride, power, wealth), Mary warns us against pride: 'He has routed those who were so proud of themselves'; against power: 'He has ousted princes from their thrones'; against wealth: 'He has sent the wealthy away empty-handed.'

As against the pseudo-grandeurs which God has confounded, Mary, still using the language of the anawim, says: 'Age after age, his care has been protecting all who fear him.' This fear is 'loving fear', full of certainty that the prayers of the poor will be heard: 'The poor man appealed and Yahweh heard and saved him' (*Ps* 34:6). And so we come to the last verse, the accomplishment of the collective salvation of Israel: 'He has come to the help of Israel his servant.'

This is the New Israel: 'Sing, O heavens, dance for joy, O

earth, for Yahweh has comforted his people and had pity on his poor!' So said Isaiah – and now it has come true. 'Ever faithful in his care for Abraham and his descendants, as long ago he promised our forefathers, he has come to the help of his servant Israel.'

The anawim are the little remnant, but the little remnant by whom the whole world is saved.

And when eventually the Son of Mary comes to gather his disciples, he, the Poor Man of poor men, even humbler than Mary among the anawim, Jesus, the poorest of the poor, will say to them: 'Blessed are the anawim, blessed are the poor!'

JESUS

The Master at prayer

And now we contemplate Jesus, the Master at prayer. And, as ever the case is with Jesus, nothing is simpler than to look at him, and yet nothing leads us into greater areas of mystery. Nothing is simpler: little Gospel phrases known to everyone, attitudes within the scope of each of us: Jesus prays, he raises his hands, he raises his eyes. Yet, nothing is more mysterious, since beyond these words and gestures we sense a crystalline world of love, of unqualified self-giving. Hence, we can never truly penetrate the prayer of Christ, except by ourselves praying and allowing Jesus to model us to his own image. But, to help us penetrate the prayer of the Son of God, of the Son of Man, let us look at the 'great' moments of his life on earth.

Nothing, you may say, bears more convincing witness to the reality of Christ's human nature than the intensity of his anguish and the intensity of his prayer.

To take his anguish first: his sorrow. The most mysterious thing about Jesus is the anguish, the distress, the anguish of which he himself says: 'There is a baptism that I must still receive, and how great my distress is until this is over!' (*Lk* 12:50). John the Beloved Disciple emphasises this throughout his Gospel. If we admit that Jesus is the Son of God, and indeed God, it is much more mysterious to see him enslaved to suffering than it is to see him transfigured. Transfiguration is his normal state. But to see him weeping over Jerusalem because the Holy City has not understood his message (*Lk* 19:41), to see him 'in great distress, sighing straight from the heart' at the sight of Martha's and Mary's grief, 'distressed and still sighing' at the tomb of Lazarus (*Jn* 11:33–38), to hear him say, 'My soul is troubled. What shall I say? Father, save me from this hour?' (*Jn* 12:27), to see him predict the treachery of one of the Twelve (*Lk* 22:21), to see him 'overcome by sadness and deep distress' (*Mt* 26:37) and finally to hear the loud cry which he uttered at the moment of death (*Mk* 15:37) – yes, this is truly mysterious for us.

The extraordinary thing, as Père de Lubac says, is not that Jesus should be God, not that God should be God, but that God should become man, in all respects like men, except in sin. And when Pilate announces: 'This is the man!' he is speaking truer than he knows. For the absolute humanity of Jesus is never more obvious than in his suffering.

But it is also obvious in his praying, which is every bit as astounding as his suffering. Gandhi gave a fine definition of prayer: 'Prayer is the daily admission of our weakness'. Now, of this weakness, Jesus gives us a daily example: a weakness chosen and admittedly voluntary, as St. Paul tells the Philippians (2:6), but nonetheless real and felt – for the entire Gospel is a veritable tissue of his prayers. We must realise that Christ's praying was continuous.

Luke shows us anguish and prayer intimately mingled in Christ's soul on the Mount of Olives, in that passage which three times mentions that he prayed 'very earnestly, in deep distress', imploring his Father to spare him the cup: 'Nevertheless, let your will be done, not mine' (*Lk* 23:39–45).

This last sentence helps us to see, given that Christ's whole life was underpinned by prayer and woven of it, that what underpinned his prayer was expressed in his saying: 'My food is to do the will of the One who sent me, and to complete his work' (*Jn* 4:34). Whatever form his prayer happened to take, that was the basis, the reason for his existence; and finishing off the work, completing the Father's work, was done by revealing himself, Jesus, and thus completing the great work begun in Abraham: the inexhaustible revelation of the Father.

'My food is to do the will of the One who sent me.' Jesus says these words to the disciples immediately after his meeting with the Samaritan woman at Jacob's Well. The food was unknown to the Apostles – as yet – although Jesus had been eating it at the moment in question. By revealing himself to the Samaritan woman, he had been accomplishing, had been

completing the Revelation: 'I who am speaking to you, I am
the Messiah' (*Jn* 4:26). The food and nourishment of Jesus
was to reveal what the gift of God was, and thus to glorify the
Father by reconciling mankind to him. When Jesus prayed, it
was always about the works that the Father had given him to
complete.

All the moments of prayer in Christ's life have to be looked
at in this light: 'My food is to do the will of the One who sent
me and to complete his work.'

The first thing that he says, in the Temple at the age of
twelve: 'Didn't you know that I must be busy with my
Father's affairs?' (*Lk* 2:50), he says actually in his Father's
House, which is a house of prayer; and there he is entirely
concerned with God. So, the force of this saying is by no
means to be under-stressed: 'I must be busy with my Father's
affairs.' It springs from the same source as those grander affir-
mations of his later years: 'My Father and I are one' (*Jn*
10:30). Even in the twelve-year-old child the same awareness
is there. And how well-linked it is to the situation of the moment. 'Your father and I have been looking for you', says
Mary. And Jesus, hearing the word father applied to Joseph,
immediately superimposes his Father – one image over the
other. 'You father and I have been looking for you.' – Ah, my
Father, that's where I ought to be, near him, in his house,
that's who I ought to be working for. He brings us, he raises
us, to the Father through his own intimacy with him. The
whole of Christ's life is an unfolding of the meaning of this
mysterious saying. Henceforward, his food consists of 'the
things of his Father'.

There is another aspect of Christ's praying that we may
consider here. Before the prayers of his public ministry, Jesus
had been a faithful little Jew! For thirty years, Jesus prayed as
Jewish child and, later, Jewish man – that is to say, incessantly! Robert Aron's *Ainsi priait Jesus enfant* (How Jesus
prayed as a child) introduces us to this unrecorded aspect of
his life. Primarily, this prayer was 'rumination', a chewing
over of the Word of God in Scripture. Christ's responses to
Satan in the wilderness before the public ministry began,
show this very clearly. Christ's soul had been fed on the Word

of God and it is enspiriting to think that, before teaching us how to pray, Jesus had himself been praying, using the same Old Testament words as we do.

Twenty years of silence follow. At 'about thirty', as the Gospel tells us, Jesus performed his first messianic gesture, a gesture surrounded by prayer and contained within a prayer. 'As he was coming out of the water,' (*Mk* 1:10), 'while he was still praying' (*Lk* 3:21), the heavens opened and he saw the Spirit in the form of a dove descending on him. There too, you observe, 'while praying'. This is the great moment, the end of the hidden, sedentary life and of his normal job, and the beginning of the great adventure of completing the entire Old Testament: 'when the times were accomplished'.

We have to understand that, when Jesus received the baptism of water, he was well aware that it would be completed by a baptism of blood, and that this first act of his public life would lead on to that final act: his Passion. Christ's prayer as he came out of the Jordan is made easier to understand by the dialogue preceding it: John the Baptist refusing to baptise Christ – since he knew or at least sensed who he was dealing with – and Jesus saying to him, 'Leave it like this for the time being. This is how we must do all that righteousness demands' (*Mt* 3:15). Notice the words 'leave it like this' and 'we must': whatever is ordained by God must be carefully carried out by John and Jesus. From this moment onwards, Christ's praying takes place in an atmosphere of complete conformity to his Father's will.

This is easily said. But when we reflect that he is a man – God-Man, of course – and hence that our human nature (shared by him) is what will be achieving this pure, this total, this supple conformity to the Father's will, we see the import of what Jesus is doing. When he is at prayer, in this prayer of conformity, at his baptism, when he proposes to do 'all that righteousness demands', behold, 'the heavens open!' 'in his own person, he has thrown down the wall of hatred and through him we have access to the Father' (cf *Ep* 2:14–16). At that moment a breach is made in the heavens: to be complemented by the Cross. The breach is already open, but the Cross will keep it so. It is, if I dare say so, a breach right into the Most High and Holy Trinity. From this moment, we penetrate the secret of God, the mystery of the Triune God. 'While Jesus, after his own baptism, was at prayer, heaven opened and the Holy Spirit descended on him, like a dove. And a voice came from heaven: "You are my Son, the Beloved; my favour rests on you" ' (*Lk* 3:21–22).

All our studies in philosophy and theology, at whatever level we may be, are actually intended to make us receptive to words like these, to events like these; and the hair-splitting *minutiae* are of great importance, in so far as these help us the better to appreciate the length and breadth, the height and depth, of what we are studying in Scripture. Having slogged over apparently very simple phrases, we shall find unsuspected depths in them: the heavens open, the Trinity appears. You see, Jesus carries the living Godhead within him, suffusing and illuminating him; at the same time, being truly man and like us in all respects save sin, he attracts the favour not only of God but of man too. His baptism is, at it were, the reassertion and increment of a quality already present in him, in his childhood and early manhood (*Lk* 2:52).

This first great moment of prayer was the first action of Christ's public life. Whenever, henceforth, he had an important decision to make, he would withdraw to the hills to lay that decision before his Father, uniting his own will to his Father's will, his prayer being entirely and exclusively this: to conform to every aspect of the Father's will.

Thus, before choosing the Twelve and proclaiming the Beatitudes, Jesus prayed, as Luke emphasises – he is the evangelist to speak most readily about Jesus at prayer: 'Now, about this time, he went out into the hills to pray and he spent the whole night in prayer to God. When day came, he summoned his disciples and picked out twelve of them' (*Lk* 6:12–13). Coming down with these, he stopped on a piece of level ground and then and there proclaimed the Beatitudes. The Lord's Prayer originated in the same way. Luke, ever faithful to Jesus as Lord of Prayer, describes how this happened: 'Now, once he was in a certain place praying. When he had finished, one of his disciples said: "Lord, teach us to pray" ' (*Lk* 11:1). Similarly, when Jesus announced that he was going to preach in Galilee, Mark tells us that 'in the morning, long before dawn, he got up, left the house and went off to a lonely place and prayed there' (*Mk* 1:35).

Given that on these occasions, Jesus was seeking the Father's will in prayer, we must not forget too that 'he could tell what a man had in him' (*Jn* 2:25); spending a night in prayer before choosing his Apostles, he already knew what was in the heart of each. He could see their rivalries, their slowness to believe (*Lk* 24:25). Christ's nights of prayer in the loneliness of the wilderness, in the seclusion of the hills, were not spent in ecstasy. The nights thus spent, before major decisions to be taken, were – as at Gethsemane – nights of anguish, at the thought of the world's salvation to be effected by the Cross.

Thus, on the night before Jesus chose the Apostles, Jesus saw Peter, whom Satan would later sift like wheat (*Lk* 22:31). Peter was to be another Job, but with a different ulcer from Job's – the ulcer of fear. For him, Jesus prayed. 'I have prayed that your faith may not fail', he later told him (*Lk* 22:32). He would have been praying for James and John too: he knew that he would be summoning them next morning, meanwhile he would have to pray for those 'Sons of Thunder' (*Mk* 3:17). John had not always been as we imagine him: which is comforting for some people to know. When John was young, he had been a bit like a thistle – thistles, as you know, prick when they're young; when they are old, they become soft, white and downy. This was the man who wanted to call down celestial fire on a village which would not open its gates to Jesus. This same young man and his brother James were to ask, 'Allow us to sit one on your right and the other on your left, in your glory' (*Mk* 10:37).

Jesus saw all this while he was praying, before these men had even made up their minds; he knew what he would have to suffer from them and with them. We could extend the list: those Apostles who were to argue among themselves as to who was the greatest (*Mk* 9:33); Thomas, who would find the truth so hard to recognise (*Jn* 20:24–25); Philip, who couldn't understand that by seeing Jesus, one saw the Father (*Jn* 14: 8–9). And then there was Judas. Judas represents us all, in differing degree, of course, at different times.

Christ's night of prayer before choosing his Apostles was therefore a night of struggle. St. Nicholas of Flue used to say, 'Praying is sometimes like going to war.' St. Paul says: 'Wrestle, fight with me in prayer.' Jesus at prayer is no stranger to the battle. True, his outward actions are enveloped in inner silence, but that inner silence is itself a battle. His inner acts at prayer prepare the way for the greatest act of all, when the Son of Man is lifted up like the brazen serpent in the wilderness (*Jn* 3:14). At prayer, Christ's orientation to the Father is inextricably linked to struggle on the human plane.

And when Christ prays, this is accompanied by very natural gestures: he climbs the mountain; he utters sighs when healing a deaf man (*Mk* 7:34); he takes the loaves and fish, raises his eyes to heaven and says a blessing over them (*Mt* 14; *Mk* 6; *Lk* 9).

Jesus never discounted or minimised the importance of supplicatory prayer. And I wonder whether, in Jesus, any distinction can be drawn between supplicatory prayer and what we call adoraton. 'We must always pray, unceasingly,' he said. In all true prayer, whether of supplication or of adoration, man opens himelf to God and receives God. The importance does not lie in the categories, whether of supplication, intercession or adoration. That is not where the scale of values is to be found, but in man's heart. Jesus asks for wonderful cures and, again, for very ordinary, material things: in each case, the gestures are the same. It is always adoration.

Whatever Jesus does, the axis of his life is revealed to us as being the Son's loving submission to his Father. Jesus set himself to live as he instructed the disciples to live: 'not by saying, "Lord, Lord!"' but by doing the will of my Heavenly Father.' And his access of joy when, 'under the action of the Holy Spirit', he 'blessed his Father', had its source in the Father's 'good pleasure' (*Lk* 10:21).

Another great moment in Christ's prayer-life was the Transfiguration. Here again, Luke gives us a much more interior description than Mark and Matthew. Here again, Jesus prays. This is mentioned twice by Luke: 'Now, about eight days afterwards, he took Peter, John and James with him and went up the mountain *to pray. As he prayed,* the appearance of his face altered and his clothes became as brilliant as lightning' (*Lk* 9:28–36). For Luke, the transfiguration witnessed by the Apostles was Christ's glory suddenly made visible. But the transfiguration was not something happening from outside; it was the visible effect of Jesus's union with the Father.

St. John does not mention the Transfiguration, but has a passage instead which scripture-scholars regard as equivalent to it, in as much as it too prepares the reader for the Passion. Just as the Transfiguration prepares the three Apostles for the shock of the Passion, so in *St. John* the passage where Jesus prepares his followers for it, has the same function. Some Greeks, who were going up to Jerusalem to worship at the festival , said to Philip: 'Sir, we should like to see Jesus.' Philip went and told Andrew; Andrew and Philip went and told Jesus. Jesus replied, ' "Now the hour has come for the Son of Man to be glorified. I tell you most solemnly, unless a wheat grain falls on the ground and dies, it remains only a single grain but if it dies, it yields a rich harvest ... Now my soul is troubled. What shall I say: Father, save me from this hour? But it was for this very reason that I have come to this hour. Father, glorify your Name!" A voice then came from heaven: "I have glorified it, and shall glorify it even more." ' (*Jn* 12:23, 27, 28). Here again, the Father's glorification of Jesus occurs in the course of a prayer and answers it: 'Father, save me from this hour ... Father, glorify your Name.'

And then there are those two short phrases, when Jesus is standing at the tomb of Lazarus. Again we see Jesus at prayer: 'Father, I thank you for having heard my prayer ... For myself, I know that you always hear me' (*Jn* 11:41). All that Jesus ever wants is this: 'My food is to do his will.' His prayer is the very humble submission of his whole being to the Father's loving will, but to a degree of identity with it that is quite beyond our powers to express. His human nature does this; our human nature can do this. These few words, 'Father, I thank you for having heard my prayer ... For myself, I know that you always hear me,' are the preface to Gethsemane and Calvary. And here again, we come on the mystery: 'For our sakes, God made the sinless one into sin, so that in him we might become divine goodness' (2 *Co* 5:21). And again, 'God put him under a curse for our sake' (*Ga* 3:13). A commentator remarks that this is one scriptural text (*Dt* 21:23) that St. Paul did not dare to transcribe as it stood, adapting it to 'under a curse *for our sake*'.

From this point on – as earlier too, but now more tensely and densely – Jesus experienced in heart and soul the totality of sin, of the world's sufferings, of the horrors of injustice: all this came flooding in at once.

I always remember something that happened one morning on the bus going from Marseilles to Saint-Maximin. It was quite early. There were half a dozen of us; there was a child, I don't know how old – about three or four, I should think, a really sweet little boy, as charming as you could imagine: gentle, forthcoming, affectionate. I don't know what could have been the matter that morning with his mother, but she was in a thoroughly bad temper. And it was really sad – nothing dramatic about it, but really sad – to see this sweet-natured, open-hearted child trying to show his affection for her and each time being repulsed. You could tell that the child was holding back his tears. Well, Christ bears the petty sufferings of a tiny child, just as much as he bears the mighty ones of freedom-fighters under torture and of murder victims. Jesus is in a state of malediction, not for any personal fault of his but by loving substitution. He has put himself under a curse. God has put him under a curse 'for our sake'. 'God made the sinless one into sin, so that in him we might become divine goodness.'

And this is the light by which we must read of Gethsemane (*Mt* 26; *Mk* 14; *Lk* 22). 'Sadness came over him and great distress. He then said to them: "My soul is sorrowful to the point of death. Wait here and keep awake with me", and throwing himself on the ground' – the physical gesture reflecting the spiritual state – 'he prayed: "Father, if it is possible, let this cup pass me by. Nevertheless, let it be as you, not I, would have it"' (*Mt* 26:37–39). You see: the shuddering, the anguish of a nature made for life, not made for death, yet bearing our sorrow and our death (*Is* 53:4).

The key to Christ's prayer in the depths of dereliction is

found in the *Epistle to the Hebrews*: 'Son as he was, he had to
learn to obey'; 'during his life on earth, he offered up prayer
and entreaty, aloud and in silent tears' – this was how Christ
prayed in Gethsemane – 'to the One who had the power to
save him from death, and he submitted so humbly that his
prayer was heard' (*Heb* 5:7–8).

And one of Christ's prayers is absolutely exceptional, in
that on earth it still goes on forever. One day, Christ's prayer
was transformed into sacrament: the Eucharist. Not only
Christ's presence with us to the end of the world, but Christ's
prayer too.

It was no accident that Jesus should have used the prayer
and commemorative meal of the Old Testament, the exodus
from Egypt and the paschal lamb (*Ex* 13). Jesus grafted his
own prayer, his all-embracing prayer-made-action, on to the
basic prayer and basic actions of the Old Covenant. On the
old stock of the olive-tree, a new olive-tree begins to sprout.
Jesus engrafts his prayer, but the prayer is not something
static; it is alive. Imagery may come to the help of words here.
Christ's prayer, the Last Supper, was like a mighty shock and
the shock-waves radiating from it, whenever the Eucharist is
celebrated, daily stir the ocean of mankind.

'Now, as they were eating, Jesus took some bread and,
when he had said the blessing' – chanted the Hallel, the divine
praises – 'he broke it and gave it to his disciples: "Take it and
eat, for this is my body." ' He gives himself up for us in an un-
ending action, an action which we can renew, an eucharist
which we can contemplate. 'And, taking the cup, he gave
thanks, prayed again and gave it to them: "Drink all of you
from this, for this is my blood, the blood of the Covenant,
which is to be poured out for many for the forgiveness of
sins" ' (*Mt* 26; *Mk* 14; *Lk* 22).

The shock wave from the first Eucharist reaches all the way
to us, every moment raising mankind on an immense, ever-in-
creasing wave of eucharistic prayer. Today, Christ celebrates
through the visible priest, but it is he celebrating nonetheless.
And the wave reaching us from the first Maundy Thursday
will carry us on to the day when 'I tell you, I shall not drink

wine until the day I drink the new wine with you in the
Kingdom of my Father' (*Mt* 26:29). This prayer-made-action,
this prayer-made-sacrament, we can make our own and by it
participate in Christ's own prayer. With him we can offer,
with him we do offer, it to the Father – what a wonderful discovery!

Finally, we penetrate the very depths of Christ in his last
great prayer: 'After saying this, Jesus raised his eyes to heaven
and said, "Father, the hour has come. Glorify your Son!"'
The twelfth chapter of *St. John's Gospel* must be read in silence;
it is the truest echo of the eternal relationship between the
Father and the Son. In verses studded with the words: Father,
Holy Father, Father, Righteous Father, Christ's great prayer
celebrates the Father's glory, Yahweh's glory. In the Old
Testament, Yahweh's glory was a dazzling splendour, the
radiant holiness and power of God present in the creation
('The heavens proclaim God's glory' – *Ps* 19:1) and in the
history of Israel ('Give thanks to Yahweh for he is good' – *Ps*
106:1).

'Father, the hour has come. Glorify your Son, so that your
Son may glorify you and, through the power over all mankind
which you have given him, may give eternal life to all those
whom you have given him. . . . Now, Father, glorify me with
the glory which I had with you before the world existed.'
With Christ, we discover that God made everything for his
glory – for our sake. For God's glory has to be reflected in our
faces, so that we, being successively transformed, can
ourselves reach God's glory (2 *Co* 3:18). The glory that Christ
wishes to give to the Father will consist for him, as man, in
walking sinlessly and docilely towards death, absolutely consenting to it and deserted by all his friends. 'Father,' – this is
the glorification which Jesus requests – 'the hour has come.
Glorify your Son so that your Son may glorify you. I have
completed the work which you gave me to do . . . My food is to
do your will.' Now the work is finished.

The completed work, forming the subject of his prayer is the
Revelation of the Father, of his Name, of Christ's true food:
'Eternal life is that they should know you, the only true God,

and your Messenger ... I have made your Name known to those whom you have taken from the world ... They were yours ... Now they know that all that you have given me comes from you.' By showing himself as Son, Jesus has made the Father known.

And, in completing his task, Jesus gives his disciples back to the Father, since here again the glory of the Father and of the disciples is one. Jesus gives several reasons for this. The first: they are yours, as they are mine. They were even yours before you gave them to me. 'I pray for them. I am not praying for the world but for those whom you have given me, because they belong to you and all I have is yours and all you have is mine, and I am glorified in them.'

So, at the moment of leaving his disciples, Jesus gives them back to his Father. They are his glory. 'I am glorified in them,' he says.

Since Jesus is about to leave them, the Father will have to look after them. They will no longer have the visible presence of his Son. 'Holy Father, keep those whom you have given me true to your Name ... I am no longer in the world; they are in the world: so that they may be one, like us. While I was with them, I kept those whom you had given me true to your Name ... except for the one who chose to be lost. But how I am coming to you and, while still in the world, I say these things to share my joy to the full with them. I have passed your word on to them and the world now hates them' – this is why the Father will have to look after them – 'because they no more belong to the world than I belong to the world. I am not asking you to remove them from the world but to protect them from the Evil One.'

Henceforth, the disciples, as extensions of Jesus, will be the Messengers. They will carry on 'and complete in their bodies what is lacking in Christ's Passion for his Church'. 'Consecrate them in the truth.' 'As you sent me into the world, so I have sent them into the world' – they will have to continue the good work – 'I pray not only for them but for all who will believe in me.' And here we see that everyone of us is included in his prayer.

And now, the final phase of his last prayer: unity in love.

After the revelation of the Father to the disciples and the committal of the disciples to the care of the Father, now comes the climax: 'May they all be one, as you, Father, are in me and I am in you, may they too be one in us, so that the world may be convinced that you sent me and that I have loved them as much as you loved me.'

If Jesus died to achieve this unity, we must not be surprised if unity among human beings is hard to achieve. We often wonder whether the game is worth the candle. There is no answer than this: 'That all may be one!' But this cost Christ his life. And then come these extraordinary words. Jesus, having spent his entire life trying to conform implicitly to the Father's will, begins to say, '*I want*': 'Father, *I want* those whom you have given me to be with me where I am, so that they may see the glory which you have given me, having loved me before the creation of the world.' Christ's prayer turns into an 'I want': 'I have revealed your Name to them so that the love with which you have loved me may be in them, and I in them.' – He means, unity in love, total communication.

TRUE BLESSEDNESS

The Word heard, kept and put into practice

A great call for air, or rather a violent blast of air is today surging through the churches of all denominations: a call to prayer. Quite unforeseen and unpredictable ten years ago when the value of prayer (was it really prayer or merely devotional exercises?) was being called into question in places where it ought most to have flourished – I mean, in seminaries and novitiates – today prayer-groups, spiritual renewal, charismatic meetings, are springing up in all directions. Prayer draws in people of all ages and conditions; barriers fall. But most important of all – and this is the real meaning of the renewal – people are now praying in the words of Scripture, and not in their own.

Now, Jesus has given us very clear indications – brief they may be, but more than ample – as to the use that we should make of the Word in our lives. And these signposts are all the more valuable to us, not for having been the subject of one of his discourses, but for having emerged from the day-to-day lives of our Lord and his immediate followers. Logically speaking therefore, we may assume that signposts arising from life will point our own prayers the way to life.

Leaving the Sermon on the Mount aside for a moment, let us consider what Jesus has to say about true blessedness. 'Now, as he was talking, a woman spoke up in the crowd and said, "Happy the womb that bore you and the breasts that you sucked!" But he replied, "Still happier they who listen to the Word of God and keep it!"' (*Lk* 11:28). *Listen and keep.*

Shortly before this incident, still in *St. Luke*, we read: 'His mother and his brothers came to see him, but they could not get to him because of the crowd. He was told, "Your mother and brothers are standing outside, and want to see you." But he replied, "My mother and my brothers are those who listen to the Word of God and put it into practice" ' (*Lk* 8:19–21). We have: *listen, keep,* and now, *listen, put into practice.*

These words echo those which we have already heard at the time of the Nativity: 'Mary for her part kept all these things in mind and pondered them in her heart,' St. Luke tells us (2:19). – *Keep in mind* and *ponder.* And he goes on: 'He went home with them to Nazareth and lived under their authority. And his mother kept all these things faithfully in her heart.' *Keep faithfully.*

Listen, keep, put into practice, keep in mind, ponder, keep faithfully: it is no accident that all these prayerful activities are attributed to, or gravitate round, the Virgin Mary, she being both the mother of the Lord and the model and mother of Christians, of disciples and of the Church. She herself is true blessedness in person, she having willingly said, 'Be it to me according to your Word!'

Listen, keep, put into practice: these three attitudes need to be observed. Each is fundamental and indispensable to prayer; there is danger in concentrating on one, or two, rather than all. Their strength lies in being all together, like the *fascis:* a sort of Trinity. Each is simple. None demands any great degree of intelligence. To understand any of these words: listen, keep, do, requires no instruction. The problem however is how not to separate them, how not to short-circuit one in favour of another. You have to keep a balance. 'What God has joined, let no man put asunder!' The quality of our lives will depend on the degree to which we keep these three aspects of prayer united. We can put up an average show, or a star performance.

To listen: etymologically, this is straightforward enough. It means to give *ear, clust* being the Welsh for ear. Listen, according to the dictionary, means to pay attention, to lend an attentive ear. Jesus tells us that, if someone wants to borrow our overcoat, we should also give him our jacket. Similarly, we must lend our brother an attentive ear, must incline our ear to him. This is what listening means.

It is an important and edifying fact that in the religion of the Old and New Testaments, hearing takes precedence over seeing. For a Christian, the ear and hearing comes before the eye and seeing. For the Greeks in New Testament times, and later for those who wanted a more intellectual, subtle and mysterious religion than the poor lower-class Christians had to offer – for those Greeks and the adepts of oriental wisdom known as Gnosis, and for those who thought of themselves as mystics: vision, seeing, took pride of place. They wanted to *see* the divine mystery, to see with both physical and intellectual eye.

Whereas in the Bible – not that there is anything wrong with seeing – the essential thing is hearing. Man's relationship to God is primarily based on hearing, on the ear: 'Faith comes from what is preached,' St. Paul says (*Rm* 10:17). This conjures up the picture of a preacher leaning forward and haranguing us from his pulpit. But it ought really to be translated as 'Faith comes from what is heard'. Faith is born of what goes into our ears, of hearing.

Why should primacy be given to hearing? Because God – we think of the satirical passages in the *Psalms* – because God is not like those dumb idols: 'They have mouths but do not speak!' Our God *has* spoken. 'Yahweh speaks.' So, listening to God is going to be the most important thing that we can do. God is the creative word of *Genesis*. He spoke and all things were made. 'He said' is the first thing that we are told about God. 'He is the living and efficacious Word,' as St. Paul says. 'The Word does not return to God empty,' Isaiah says in that well-known passage (53:11). 'As the rain and the snow come down from the sky and do not return without watering the earth, without achieving their effect of giving bread to the farmer, so my Almighty Word will not return to me – Yahweh says – without having achieved its task.'

And when St. John begins the marvellous prologue to his *Gospel:* 'In the beginning was the Word,' he intends to show that what had been already said in *Genesis* and in *Isaiah* has now come true in the Living Word, who is Jesus Christ.

Our relationship with God is indeed a mouth-to-ear one. Jeremiah and Amos never stop saying, 'Listen!', 'Yahweh's word'. The Wise-man in the *Proverbs* says, 'Listen, my son!' and devout Israelites repeat to this day, 'Listen, O Israel, the Lord your God is one!' When Jesus begins preaching in parables, he says, 'Listen!' And at the end, he adds, 'He who has ears to hear, let him hear!' All the time, listening. And the Apostle James says, 'Let each man be ready to listen!' This is the leitmotiv of the Bible.

Listen, then — but what does that mean? First, keep quiet. Secondly, be at God's disposal. Thirdly, open your heart. But even taken in three stages, this is one and the same response to God when he knocks at the soul. It is the response of the *Song of Songs:* 'See, how my Beloved comes, leaping through the darkness across the hills', and he knocks on my door. It is the response of the *Book of Revelation* (3:20), 'Look, I am standing at the door, knocking. If anyone opens the door, I shall come in to share his meal.' It is also the response in the parable of the Ten Virgins: 'See, now the Bridegroom comes to the door and knocks.' Listening is the response to God's action of knocking: it implies opening the door, being ready to open the door.

To take the three requisites . . . First, silence. This looks like a statement of the obvious: listening and keeping quiet are more or less the same thing. All the same, we must re-emphasise: silence is our way of helping God, so that he can come to us; silence is the calming and settling of the turgid waters: silence is one of man's physiological necessities. Muscular life needs movement and exercise; spiritual life needs silence. Not inaction, but inner silence. Not at all a rigid, obligatory silence, not a forced silence, but a language preparing the way for love. The very silence of Christ, the visible expression of the Eternal Word. St. John of the Cross tells us in two lines how deep that silence is: 'The Father says a word; it is his Word and it is his Son. He says it in eternal silence and in silence the soul hears it.'

Secondly, being at God's disposal. This means nearly the same thing, but it takes us a little further. The Word of God can only enter empty, stripped-down souls. A rich man finds it hard to be available. He has too many worries, too many things to do: the car to buy, the telephone out of order, the refrigerator to be changed, the stock exchange going down, gold shares going up! This is why it is harder for a rich man to enter the Kingdom than for a camel to go through the eye of a needle. He owns too many things; his heart, his mind and his senses are all over-burdened.

The Word enters souls which are no longer encumbered by their own capabilities, but which are not encumbered by their incapabilities either. It is certainly tiresome to be encumbered by capabilities, but that has its consolations! To be encumbered by one's incapabilities is a disaster: 'I'm no good', 'this won't turn out right' and so on. If one is empty, one is no more encumbered by incapabilities than by abilities. The Word is received by those who wait and call. Why did the Athenians tell St. Paul, their missionary, to go and boil his head? Athens was the most open-minded place in the world: philosophy flourished there, there were universities, marvellous libraries; it was a noble, intellectual civilisation. The intellect is not to be decried. And in Athens, in contrast to Corinth, there was a moral culture too. People loved order, beauty, harmony: there was no intolerance. It was an open society. What upset the wise men of Athens was not, in the final analysis, a detail of doctrine, the resurrection, – for they had heard stranger things than that. Père Festugière says: 'What prevented them from accepting Paul's teaching was their own basic cast of mind. They listened' – yes, they listened alright – 'but only as dilettantes, curious to know what he would say, but with no desire to learn.' The desire to learn is frequently mentioned in the Bible. As far as they were concerned, Paul was bringing them one more philosophic system, possibly worth discussing – but that was all. They were not available.

Whereas the people of Corinth – the Greek word, 'Corinthianise' meant expressively enough 'to be a loose woman' – the porters and prostitutes of Corinth, more coarse-grained and certainly more besmirched than the people of Athens, were also much newer. These people were available; none of them felt inclined to say, 'We know all this already.' It didn't occur to them to make comparisons or to start arguing. Listening doesn't merely mean being empty, but being ready to receive.

Lastly: opening the heart. Opening the heart follows on
from the two attitudes above, when God's grace seizes on it. I
can listen, I can even try to be empty, but God is the one who
will open my heart. Here, we must look at two very meaty
verses in the *Acts of the Apostles,* describing the conversion of
Lydia at Philippi in Macedonia:

'We went along the river, outside the gates, as it was the
Sabbath, to the customary place of prayer. We sat down and
preached to the women who had come to the meeting. One of
them, called Lydia, a devout woman from the town of
Thyatira, who was in the purple-dye trade, was all ears, the
Lord having opened her heart to make her receptive to what
Paul was saying' (*Ac* 16:13–14).

You have it all there: listening (she was all ears), the result
of listening (the Lord had opened her heart) and the need for
someone to speak (the words of Paul). Moses said, 'God has
given us a heart, to know him' (cf. *Dt* 29:3).

The second basic need is to keep the Word, to preserve and
ponder it.

With Lydia All-Ears, we can see that 'listening' leads immediately to 'keeping', 'pondering'. Claudel, that earthquake
of a poet, with great insight remarks, 'Many wise men have
told us that, in order to hear, it would probably be enough
were we to listen. How true! But now, not with our faculty of
hearing, not even with our straining intellect, but with our
very being, we listen to Existence existing.'

'Keeping the Word' is precisely this burying within
ourselves, this sowing within ourselves, not of mere words, but
of the life of the Word of God. This is the parable of the Sower:
but perhaps it is less about the quality of the soil – which is us
– whether good or stony, than about duration. Not so much
about the capacity to receive, as about the capacity to retain
what is sown. The birds of heaven and the feet of passers-by
destroy the grain as soon as sown; where the soil is poor, the
grain sprouts quickly but then dries out for lack of moisture:
this is your man 'who doesn't last', as Jesus says (*Mk* 13:21).
In soil overgrown with brambles, the Word germinates and
takes root, but though it starts growing, it 'gets choked on the

way' and doesn't reach maturity (*Lk* 8:14). Through these graduations of durability, we finally come to the good soil: the people who with noble and generous heart, have heard the Word, hold on to it and yield a harvest, thanks to their perseverance (*Lk* 8:15). The season has run full course. And Mark adds — and only he — the parable of the seed which sprouts without anyone's having done anything about it; 'day and night' it develops. Jesus describes the stages: the grain germinates and sprouts, it comes up green; next, the ear; then ears full of wheat (*Mk* 4:26–29).

So, once the Word has been heard, we have to make it stay in us, not sterilising it as in a cold-store, but letting it grow through the successive stages of our life. The cold-storage happens when the papers and books come between the Word and us, as in the poem written by Josef Reding for the Synod of the Federal German Catholic Church:

Lord,
they take it in turns
to slip bits of paper
between you
and me.

I am afraid
I soon shan't be able
to see you.

Could a spark
of your spirit
set fire
to these papers,
do you think?

And above this gray
crumpled mass
make you visible
once more?

And what does the word ponder mean to us? Shutting our eyes, furrowing our foreheads and forcing ourselves to come up with some idea of our own? But in Hebrew, the word for pondering or meditating has the primary meanings of murmuring, complaining, divulging, speaking, and hence of pondering and meditating. Meditation is a state of total contemplative receptivity in which a man murmurs the Torah, reciting it to himself in a low voice. The Eternal Word of the Eternal One is not meant to be kept in a bullet-proof glass case in a museum like Leonardo da Vinci's *Mona Lisa;* but to be treated as a peasant treats his wheat, plunging his hand into it, letting it run through his fingers, to admire it and so assert his ownership of it.

An immense number of psalms make this same point. Psalm 1, the preface to the whole *Psalter,* introduces the subject:

> How blessed the man who has not joined
> 　　the council of the wicked,
> nor stood in the assembly of sinners,
> nor sat in the session of the sceptics,
> but who finds his pleasure in the law of Yahweh,
> 　　murmuring that over, day and night!

Or again, Psalm 63:

> When on my bed I think of you
> 　　and through my vigils muse on you,
> may my soul cling close to you,
> 　　may your right hand clasp me!

Or again, Psalm 57:

> I shall make full tally of your works
> 　　while speaking of your mighty deeds.

The meditative murmur rises to a cry of distress in moments of crisis, Psalm 28:

> Yahweh, to you I call,
> 　　my Rock, do not say nothing!

There is a time for meditating and a time for calling for help, Psalm 5:

> O Yahweh, give my words a hearing,
>   listen to what I say,
> listen to my call for help,
>   my King and my God!

But the most significant thing about being on guard in prayer – as one might say of a sentry guarding one of the enemy's objectives – is the 'act of remembering'. Jesus uses the expression and it is repeated at each celebration of the Eucharist. This doesn't mean getting something by heart, or remembering something already past and gone, but making the event go on, making it come alive today, making the Word become present and real. Giving the Word new life. The Word, first said by the Psalmist, takes on new life in me when I murmur it and when I make the event in question come alive again. 'Do this in memory of me' ought to be rendered: 'Do this as my memorial', like a monument, making someone or something present and real before God and man. Thus, 'to remember' commits us to action.

In *La Vie quotidienne des Hebreux* (Daily life of the Ancient Hebrews), Chouraqui explains that Western man has a very different notion of time from that of the Ancient Hebrews. To understand one important aspect of prayer, we have to enter their mentality. For a Hebrew and for the people of the Bible, the time at which an action takes place – whether in the past, the present or the future – which we consider essential to know, 'is only of secondary importance for a Hebrew and never expressed'. The important thing is that an event (in the past) re-exists at the moment when it is expressed in words. 'The Hebrew sentence describes situations and each word projects an image. The sentence unwinds like a film, each letter of the text, each accent, each breathing, each silence being so many constituent elements.' In a word, we in the West site events in relation to ourselves, hence the importance of past, present and future. Looking at a war memorial, I think of the sacrifice made by those heroes *of the past*. The Semite, in contrast, participates in the event as a present reality, like St. Paul. He joins in the race, runs for all he is worth. He will not settle for being a spectator. And this makes his prayer active and effective. Instead of intellectual speculations: this is what happened three thousand years ago at the Exodus; was it three thousand or four thousand years ago? ... the Hebrew lives the Exodus, he is at this moment in the Exodus. And if he doesn't grasp the significance of an event (past or present to us), he knows that what is now incomprehensible will at some point in the race become comprehensible (although not now). This is the meaning underlying Luke's words about Mary: 'Mary, for her part, kept all these things in mind and pondered them in her heart' (*Lk* 2:19).

A similar formula occurs in *Genesis:* 'Joseph's brothers were jealous of him, but his father kept the thing' – Joseph's dream – 'in mind' (37:11); as also in *Daniel*, after Daniel's vision: 'I was greatly disturbed in my thoughts, my expression changed and I kept these matters in my heart.' The expression means that the recipient of a revelation keeps it for the future. He doesn't understand what it means at the time, but he knows that at a given moment of the race there will be an explanation for what is happening now. He lives in the present. Thus, Luke stresses Mary's reflecting on facts, the meaning of which will not be clearly seen until the Easter Revelation. Only then will what she has been reflecting on and keeping in her heart like a living thing, be explained.

We are miles away from intellectual reconstructions of events. Meditating means mingling in the crowd, ever more or less hopeful of seeing Jesus work a miracle. Meditating on the arraignment of Jesus means going into Pilate's judgment-hall, not as a spectator, but as a witness, or even as a judge who will have to answer for condemning Jesus to death. Meditating means being part of 'the cloud of witnesses' filling the pages of the Bible. And the only way of finding out whether or not these witnesses are right is to expose ourselves to the action of the Bible. Many things remain which we cannot understand, we shall not be able to assimilate everything, but we shall meet one person who demands a decision from us: Jesus. We shall see Jesus from the same point of view as the one from which the Evangelists and Apostles saw him.

Now, if 'listening' and 'keeping the Word' mean reliving these events and allowing them to transform us, this is already 'putting the Word into practice'. We understand why and how the 'contemplatives' of the Bible are active. With them, we are fully involved in the problems and struggles of this life. But the problems and struggles have first to be experienced in the depths of the heart; only then can they be carried onto the battlefields of common life. When we listen, when we meditate, when we murmur through the years: 'He who would be my disciple, let him take up his cross each day and follow me'; when the two words 'his cross' *my* cross, my personal one, then 'each day and follow me' have been murmured over and meditated on: they will throw light on my own situation. They are no longer vague, but words becoming the watchwords of my life: absorbed into my blood and bone, if I myself am true; or recognised as a vital need and yearned for with all my being, if I am unfaithful to them. This helps us to understand what is meant by the double-edged sword in the *Epistle to the Hebrews:* 'The Word of God is alive, energetic and sharper than any double-edged sword.' Double-edged, 'so that it can strike forwards to cut down obstacles, or backwards to quell resistance' (Claudel). Just so, that's what the two edges do. The Word is so sharp, it can divide soul from spirit; it tests the thoughts and motives of the heart. This, you can see, is no ordinary listening, but something growing in us as in the parable. 'No created thing can escape his sight, everything is naked to his eye, everything is subject to his gaze' (*Heb* 4:13). The Greek word is even more graphic: everything is 'mastered, being seized by the neck', as a wrestler catches his opponent by the neck and makes him helpless.

And here we can turn to Madeleine Delbrêl. This is why: she wasn't a nun, nor a specialist in religion or psychology, but a social worker immersed in the thousand and one activities and pre-occupations of her job, leading an ordinary life with ordinary activities, as a Christian. So where does the grace come from, transforming her life into prayer? Where does she get her outlook, guiding her through the intricacies of the world? One day, she wrote this – for herself. It doesn't need a commentary. This is how a contemporary heard, kept and practised the Gospel, the 'Lord's Book', as she called it:

The Gospel is the book of the Lord's life. It was written to be the book of our lives.

It wasn't written to be understood, but to be approached like a mysterious threshold.

It wasn't written to be read, but to be absorbed.

Each of its words is spirit and life. Agile and free, they only await our spiritual hunger, to fuse with our soul. Living, they are like leaven, seizing on our dough and making it ferment with a new type of life.

The words of human books can be understood and weighed.

The words of the Gospel are experienced and borne.

We assimilate the words in books. The words of the Gospel mould, alter and, you might say, assimilate us.

When Jesus tells us: 'Do not reclaim what you have lent', or, 'Yes, yes, no, no: everything else is from the Evil One', we are being asked merely to obey . . . and arguing will not help us to do so.

What will help us is to carry, to 'keep' – in the warmth of our faith and hope – the word that we want to obey. Between it and our will, a sort of pact for life will be cemented.

Whenever we hold the Gospel in our hands, we ought to think that in it lives the Word who wants to become flesh in us, to capture us, so that, with his heart grafted on to ours and with his spirit plugged into our spirit, we can begin his life again, in another place, in another age, in another human society.

Putting the Gospel into practice like this means renouncing our own lives, to receive a destiny none other than Christ himself.

ST. PAUL

'To live is Christ'

There are many, many lines of approach to the thought and prayer of St. Paul. I suggest two phrases to you. The first, uttered by Jesus, was the one that triggered off St. Paul's conversion. He was on the way to Damascus to hunt out, arrest and send back 'in chains' to Jerusalem, those who were disciples of the Lord. Hearing the voice saying to him, 'Saul, Saul, why are you persecuting me?' he asked, 'Who are you, Lord?' Came the answer, turning his life inside out: 'I am Jesus and you are persecuting me' (*Ac* 9:5). These few words of Jesus, so sharp and clear, lodged forever in Paul's heart.

The other phrase is one of Paul's himself: 'Woe to me, if I do not preach the Gospel' (1 *Co* 9:16). The word he uses, 'Woe!' was the one used by the spectators when a gladiator looked like being beaten: *Vae victis!* (woe to the vanquished!). 'Woe to me', something terrible will happen to me if I do not proclaim the Gospel. And St. Paul elaborates: 'Not that I boast of preaching the Gospel, since it is a necessity laid on me. But woe to me, were I not to preach it!' He uses, furthermore, the word 'necessity' which in Greek tragedies of his day covered everything unavoidable in one's destiny: *ananke*. It is a necessity, I can't do anything else. Woe then to me!

These two phrases form the preparation and framework for St. Paul's prayer. The conversion phrase was the source of his two fundamental discoveries, the first being the universality of the Body of Christ: 'There are no distinctions between Jew and Greek, slave and free, male and female, but all of you are one in Christ Jesus' (*Ga* 3:28). Thus, the Kingdom, the Body of Christ, embraces all mankind, transcending all social and other categories.

St. Paul's second great discovery was that salvation is attained by faith in Jesus Christ and not by the Law. And we have to keep this very much in mind if we are to grasp the essential characteristics of Paul's apostolic and evangelical prayer. This theme recurs in all his letters: 'For him, Jesus Christ my Lord, I have accepted the loss of everything, and I look on everything as so much rubbish' – floor-sweepings – 'if only I can have Christ and be given a place in him. I am no longer trying for perfection by my own efforts, that perfection which comes from the Law,' – observances – 'but I want only the perfection which comes through faith in Christ, and is from God and based on faith. All I want is to have Christ and the power of his resurrection, and to share his sufferings' (*Ph* 3:8–10). In Paul, salvation by faith in Jesus Christ and not by the Law shows the primacy of the inward over the outward. Jesus had said, 'Nothing that goes into a man from outside can make him unclean; it is what comes out of a man that makes him unclean' (*Mk* 7:15). The primacy of the Spirit over the letter: the Spirit gives life, the letter kills. The primacy of the life of grace over external observances. All this leads us to the essence of prayer – the primacy of purity of heart over purifications prescribed by law, and the primacy of faith over works. Even so, St. Paul scorns nothing, suppresses nothing. He is still 'a Hebrew born of Hebrew parents' and, as regards the Law, a Pharisee (*Ph* 3:5), but everything, whether sacred or profane, everything becomes the field of inner sanctification by the Spirit: 'Whatever you eat, whatever you drink, whatever you do, do all for the glory of God' (1 *Co* 10:31).

Owing to these two intuitions – if the basis of his life is free election, call and vocation coming from God, if his fulcrum and assurance is that he is an 'Apostle by the grace of God' and not by works – for him, the lever by which he will lift the world can only be prayer. For Paul, prayer is not an exercise to be performed, nor is it simply an encounter with God – I say 'simply' as though this were something simple! – but the direct result of his discovery of Jesus Christ on the road to Damascus: it is apostolic.

What are the outstanding characteristics of Paul's prayer? The first, practised by Paul and insistently emphasised to everyone else is the saying of Jesus recorded by Luke: 'Then Jesus told them a parable about the need to pray continually and never lose heart' – the parable of the widow and the judge who didn't want to listen to her (*Lk* 18:1). And interestingly, there is a link between Luke and Paul here, for Luke's phrasing ('He told them a parable about the need to pray continually') was borrowed from Paul.

To pray continually, never to lose heart: these five words summarise Christ's entire teaching. Jesus did not leave us a treatise on prayer, but he did say, 'Persevere in prayer'. The first Christians remembered what Jesus had taught them: 'They were perseverant in prayer.' And the first thing that Paul reminds us to do – and we learn this from his life, since he didn't write a treatise on prayer either – is: 'Pray without ceasing.' As Jesus said, it's the continuity of prayer that counts. We must never tire of re-reading the passages in which Paul repeats that we must pray continually and never lose heart. The word continually recurring in his letters is this very word 'continually'. 'Pray continually.' 'Pray at all times.' 'Pray night and day.' 'Pray every moment.'

Here are a few references. To the Romans (*Rm* 1:9–10): 'Without ceasing I remember you, always petitioning in my prayers . . .' Paul was not influenced by that style known as ecclesiastical, whether cultivated in seminaries or in the bureaucracy of the Church. Yet he writes: 'Without ceasing I remember you, always petitioning in my prayers . . .' So, if he said it, it must have been true, and not very exaggerated, even though he was a Mediterranean type.

'Brothers', he says, still writing to the Romans, 'my heart's desire and prayer to God for them is that they may be saved' (*Rm* 10:1). The prayer is truly his heart's desire, it is ceaseless since it comes from the heart; his very heart beats to this rhythm. 'I never cease to thank God for you and to remember you in my prayers' (*Ph* 1:3).

At the heart of this continuity, of this ceaseless prayer, are two things invariably intermingling in St. Paul: supplication and praise. For Paul, though they are two different things, they are in reality one and the same: what he himself calls 'prayer suffused with thanksgiving'. Listen to what he says to the Philippians: 'I thank my God' – I give thanks, i.e. praise, joy – 'whenever I remember you, always in my prayers for all of you petitioning joyfully' (1:3–4).

You see how Paul's apostolic supplication is always linked to praise.

Further on, he says even more specifically, 'In every need, by prayer and supplication with thanksgiving make your requests known to God' (*Ph* 4:6). This is important, because this is what will give us joy. If we had only requests and supplications to put forward, we should end up by being tense, gloomy and very unattractive. Whereas the prayer, the request, the supplication practised by Paul is ever lively and joyfully made. This is St. Paul's secret: the mixing of appeal and joy, even when he is actually suffering: 'We never stop giving thanks to God, Father of our Lord Jesus Christ, and thinking of you in our prayers' (*Col* 1:3). This is important: he is never content to pray, but must give thanks to God, like the leper, the only leper to come back of the ten who had been healed, the only one to thank God for his cure. When Paul prays, he gives thanks at the same time.

What Jesus says: 'Father, I thank you, for I know that you always hear me' (*Jn* 11:41–42), Paul repeats, and we can repeat it too. And again: 'We thank God at all times for you all when we remember you in our prayers' (1 *Th* 1:3). Joy and praise ever fill his heart.

You could say that in St. Paul thanksgiving acts as a magnet to the other constituent elements of his prayer. All are contained in and enriched by thanksgiving. Because of what we have received once and for all in Jesus Christ – 'if you only knew what God is offering you' (*Jn* 4:10) – we have an inexhaustible reason for giving thanks. Henceforth, all prayer must have thanksgiving for its starting-point.

It is typical that the collection for the Church of Jerusalem – a very material thing, an exercise in fund-raising for the Church – should itself have been a source of thanksgiving for Paul: 'Your generous deeds will be a cause of thanksgiving to God' (2 *Co* 9:11).

Thus, supplication and praise for Paul are woven into a single prayer.

Let us also hear what he has to say to the Thessalonians: 'How can we thank God enough for you' – thanksgiving – 'for all the joy we feel before our God on your account? We are earnestly praying night and day' – continuity in prayer – 'to be able to see you face to face again and make up any short-comings in your faith' (1 *Th* 3:9–10). Paul does not disregard supplicatory prayer; he wants to see those beloved faces again, he is athirst to visit his beloved Thessalonians. This must be emphasised: not only does he not devalue supplicatory prayer, but he makes requests for himself; he does not hesitate to pray for himself, for the thorn in his flesh – that enigmatic condition – implanted in him: 'Three times, I have pleaded with the Lord to remove the thorn in my flesh.' He does pray for himself, but his prayer is not granted, since the Lord answers, 'My grace is sufficient for you.' Paul's prayers often have been heard, but on this occasion they are not – humanly speaking at least: 'My grace is enough for you; my power is at its best in weakness' (2 *Co* 12:8–9). It is hard on him to be refused, but if this is the way that God's power is to be manifested, Paul rejoices just the same: 'And that is why I am content with my weaknesses . . . for when I am weak, that is when I am strong' (2 *Co* 12:10).

His prayer of thanksgiving leads him to ask for whatever is needful for the salvation of all: whether it be the collection, or to see friends face to face. And this prayer turns into a 'memorial'. This is another very typical expression of Paul's: he 'makes a memorial'. In the Jewish religion of the day, 'making a memorial' was a most important religious act: a re-enactment of a past event, making it present again. This is so deeply fixed in Paul's heart that he spontaneously 'memorialises' his brothers, re-actualising his brothers' memory. To Timothy, he writes, 'I give thanks' – this is ever part of his prayer – 'I give thanks to God whom with a pure conscience I serve, as my forefathers did,' – here again, he memorialises his ancestors – 'when without ceasing, night and day' – continuity! – 'I memoralise you in my prayers' (2 *Tm* 1:3).

He gladly memorialises people, making them live again in himself. Even in his short note to Philemon, he says, 'I thank

my God continually, memorialising you in my prayers.'
Again, St. Paul's continuity in prayer.

The second characteristic of St. Paul's prayer is that it is
apostolic: bound up with the mystery of Christ and the Gospel
which he has discovered and is determined to proclaim. For
Paul, prayer and apostolic activity are indivisible. For him,
therefore, praying means struggling, fighting. It is very
remote, therefore, from sugary effusions or self-consciously
elegant songs of praise – not that singing isn't a fine way of
praising God, as the psalmists make so clear – no, for Paul,
since his prayer is apostolic, it is primarily a battle. 'Struggle
with me in the prayers which you offer to God on my behalf'
(*Rm* 15:30).

He encourages the Colossians by reminding them that he is
not alone, that other brothers have grasped the same point:
'Epaphras is constantly struggling for you in his prayers' (*Col*
4:12).

The struggle is waged on behalf of everyone. In the same
epistle, Paul tells them about his own apostolic struggle: 'I
want you to know what a tough fight I am putting up for you,
for the Laodicaeans and for all sorts of other people who have
never actually seen me' (*Col* 2:1). The apostolic life is one long
fight, but prayer is the source, as also the weapon, in this
apostolic struggle.

If apostolic prayer is a fight, a struggle, this is because it is a
form of child-bearing. It is the bringing to birth of the Body of
Christ by preaching, by the proclamation of the Good News:
'You have only one father who begot you in Christ' (cf. 1 *Co*
4:15). And again, he writes to the Galatians: 'My little
children, I must go through the pain of giving birth to you over
again, until Christ is formed in you' (4:19).

There is also that very strange passage in *Thessalonians*,
where Paul compares himself simultaneously to a father and
to a mother: 'As God is my witness, we never tried to impress
you. On the contrary, we behaved in a very unassuming way
when we were with you.' – His unassuming behaviour fitted
him perfectly to be their father and mother. – 'Like a mother
feeding and looking after her children,' – there is a maternal
aspect in Paul's child-bearing of Christ in his converts – 'we

felt so devoted and protective towards you and had come to love you so much, that we were eager to hand over to you not only the Good News but our whole lives as well. Let me remind you how hard we used to work,' – like a mother whose work is never done, he has to get up at night as well as in the morning – 'slaving night and day so as not to be a burden to any of you.' At the same time, Paul is like a father. 'You can remember how we treated every one of you as a father treats his children,' – if the mother represents tenderness, the father is head of the family nonetheless – 'exhorting you,' – encouraging, assuring and possibly bawling at them – 'to live a life worthy of God, who is calling you to share the glory of his Kingdom' (1 *Th* 5:7–12).

St. Paul's prayer is thus a struggle, a child-bearing. On another occasion, he says, 'Thus death labours in us, and life in you' (1 *Co* 4:12). St. John says much the same: 'If anyone sees his brother commit a sin, he has only to pray and God will give life to the sinner' (1 *Jn* 5:16). The brother's life depends on prayer; John too has experienced this.

Here, I feel I must digress. I am not against this or that; but with regard to the things of God, these are so immense and so far beyond us that they emphatically cannot be measured by the same standards as human activities, however excellent the latter may be. This said, we must understand that methods and techniques of any kind you care to mention: zen, yoga, lotus – none of these is a substitute for the blazing incandescence of a heart afire with love. It is just because Paul, as father and as mother, endures the pangs of childbirth for Christ and the members of the Body of Christ, that his prayer is so tremendously strong. If we devote our time to methods and techniques, we shall never get off the ground.

What we do have to do is try and kindle the flame in the heart. Without that, we shall fall back into observances, which is what Paul does not want. What is the difference between a mother-wolf howling over the corpse of her wolf-cub, and an undertaker shaking hands with you, holding his bill behind his back while he offers you his condolences? Prayer is heat, prayer is the howling wolf. Our objective has to be this: to kindle the blaze in our heart. Then prayer will have some vitality.

Prayer is as strong as the passion inspiring it. 'Nothing can come between us and the love of Christ. For of this I am certain: neither death nor life, nor any created thing, tribulation, anguish, hunger – can come between us and the love of God made visible in Christ Jesus' (*Rm* 8:35–39).

When Paul proclaims his faith, his certainty, in terms like these, he doesn't need a method: he is on fire. But his child-bearing is not in isolation – if I may put it thus. Paul asks for his brothers' prayers, and each time he asks his brothers to pray that the Gospel may be preached to all. So that the 'Woe to me if I do not proclaim the Gospel' may be averted. 'Brothers, pray for us, pray that the Lord's message may spread quickly' (2 *Th* 3:1). And again, to the Ephesians (6:19): 'Pray for me to be given an opportunity to open my mouth.'

In the church of St. Trophime at Arles in Provence, there is a very ancient statue of St. Paul, eroded by time, a very old statue indeed. The only part of it intact is the mouth. The nose is broken, the ears have come off, but the open mouth is all the more impressive for being the only feature left. A fine illustration of what St. Paul was asking the Ephesians to do: 'Pray for me to be given an opportunity to open my mouth, to speak and boldly to proclaim the mystery of the Gospel, of which I am an ambassador in chains. Pray that, in proclaiming it, I may speak as boldly as I should.' This is the Apostle's request, his prayer and what he wants his brothers to pray for.

Third characteristic of Paul's prayer. Here we can't put a title since what we have is a paradox. To the Romans, for instance, he says, 'My sorrow is so great, my mental anguish so endless, that I would willingly be excommunicated, if that would help my brothers.' He is in the midst of the struggle and is suffering as he struggles. At the same time – here is the paradox – the man who suffers incessantly, as incessantly as he prays, can also say, 'My joy overflows in the midst of all my troubles' (2 *Co* 7:4). I once heard this said by someone else, Paul VI, and it was like St. Paul coming back to life. We were having a private conversation. The Pope was talking about his troubles, which in his case are the Church's troubles. He wasn't telling me about whether or not he was suffering from arthritis, but about the problems and worries of the Church. 'All the same,' he went on, 'there are fine things in the Church today.' And suddenly his face lit up and he said, 'Oh, yes, my joy overflows in the midst of these troubles, when I see all these fine things.' For a moment, I couldn't be sure whether I was listening to Paul VI or to St. Paul himself.

The paradox about St. Paul lies precisely in this mixture of suffering and joy. 'It makes me happy to suffer for you,' as I am suffering now, and in my own body to do what I can to make up what still has to be undergone by Christ for the sake of his Body, the Church. This is why I struggle wearily on, with his' – i.e. Christ's – 'power irresistibly driving me' (*Col* 1:24–29). This is doing what the Lord said: 'that one had to pray all the time, never allowing oneself to be discouraged, never getting tired of doing it.' This is St. Paul's theme throughout his letters: to the Corinthians, the Galatians, the Thessalonians, the Ephesians: 'For your part, brothers, never get tired of doing good.' – Don't say, 'Heavens, I'm sick of that!' – 'This is why, mysteriously entrusted with this ministry, there is no weakening on our part' (2 *Co* 4:1). And again: 'This is why we do not lose courage, and never get tired of doing what is right' (*Ga* 6:9; 2 *Th* 3:13). To the Ephesians, he says (3:13): 'So I beg you, never lose confidence, just because of the trials which I go through.'

Here we are, back among the Old Testament virtues: *hesed*, a word habitually applied to God, but also used to denote the virtue of a man of prayer. Old Testament *hesed* is the attachment of someone for someone else, with the implied meaning of mutual help, of active and faithful devotion. Hence, from God's side, God's compassionate love for Israel, his first-born. But, from man's side, a loving nearness, a nearness both loving and fearful, fearful in the sense of not wanting to do anything to displease the one whom he loves. This is the atmosphere of prayer for Paul.

The *hassid*, or man who lives in the atmosphere and state of prayer, feels an attachment to God consisting of tenderness and respect combined. The words 'affection', 'love', 'worship', all meet in this. The basic sense of tender attachment to God is what transfigures all the obligations of Christian life in the light of the mystery of God's love for us.

Such is the scope of the virtue from the human side. And Christ is the image, the perfect ikon of God's *hesed*, as also of *hesed* at its most developed in man. But how would one translate this? I'm afraid that the word normally used falls far short of the mark.

St. Paul uses a special word for it, a Greek word: *eusebia*, which is rendered, for want of a better expression, as 'mystery of piety'. But piety here means something entirely different from a nice, pious nun lighting candles and neatly genuflecting. We have worn the word piety out: 'She's a pious little thing!' And this isn't saying much! We shall have to restore it to truer proportions. Piety, for St. Paul, is the basic climate of prayer, with charity, of course. St. Paul talks about piety all through the pastoral epistles. There are texts aplenty: 'To lead the elect of God to faith and knowledge of the truth ordered by piety.' And again, to Timothy: 'so that we may be able to lead calm and peaceful lives in all piety and dignity' (1 *Tm* 2:2).

There is no question of pious exercises: piety is a climate. Paul tells Timothy: 'Train yourself to piety' (1 *Tm* 4:7), as being one of the essential things that he must do. Again, forget any sentimental associations that the word my have for you. 'Piety,' says St. Paul, 'holds out the reward of life here and now and of the future life as well. Its usefulness is unlimited . . . Doing this, you will save both yourself and those who listen to you' (1 *Tm* 8–16). You see the point: the word has to be restored to the climate of *hesed.* The pious man of the Old Testament is the one who believes in the One God and who relies on him alone. He is one of the *anawim.*

Here is how Père Spicq describes the climate of 'piety': one believes in a holy, almighty, loving God; one respects him, one 'fears' him, one loves him, one submits to him absolutely, one makes one's own will conform to his and one keeps his commandments – not out of fear but with the intention of honouring him. All moral, all human, life becomes worship, becomes religious service. And the peak, for St. Paul, is Christ, 'the mystery of piety' he says.

This piety colours all our life and all our actions. For Paul, it has two consequences. First, it frees a man from the love of gain, it detaches him from earthly goods, from the lure of possessions. In the letters to Timothy, Paul frequently returns to this: 'This is what you are to teach them to believe and persuade them to do . . . the doctrine concordant with piety . . . Piety does bring large profits to him who is content with what he has . . . As long as we have food and clothing, let us be content with that; people who long to be rich are a prey to temptation; they get trapped' (1 *Tm* 6:3–10).

Furthermore, piety is the climate and soil in which prayer takes root. Piety gives us strength to overcome opposition. 'You know,' Paul says to Timothy on another occasion, 'what I have taught . . . You are well aware, then, that those who try to live in Christ with piety' – with those overtones already described – 'will be persecuted' (2 *Tm* 3:10–12). While the others, Paul says, are 'sinners and charlatans'. Thus, piety leads the Apostle to detachment from the world, and gives him the strength to surmount opposition.

Why must all apostolic life be impregnated by prayer? There are at least five reasons:

First: because Christ alone makes things grow. Paul has planted, someone else has watered, but Paul and Apollos are only fellow-workmen, gardeners; God alone makes the things grow (1 *Co* 3:5–11). They are the architects, but there is no other foundation than Jesus Christ. We pray, because only Jesus Christ can make the apostolic work thrive, and make the grain germinate.

The second reason is as follows: 'so that faith should depend on the power of God and not on human philosophy. What we teach, in contrast, is the hidden, mysterious wisdom of God' (1 *Co* 2:5–7). This sort of wisdom only God can give: before other types of wisdom, Paul would be floored and at a loss.

Third reason: 'For it is not against human enemies that we have to fight', not merely against men promoting the merits of this or that political system. Fights of this sort are only signs and symbols, the visible aspect of what is invisible. 'It is not against human enemies that we have to fight, but against the

Spirits of Evil' (*Ep* 6:12).

Fourth reason: 'For we are the ministers of Christ to the pagans.' Here lies Paul's invincible strength: 'I write boldly . . . because God has given me the privilege of being a minister of Christ Jesus to the pagans, a priest of God's Gospel, to make the pagans acceptable as an offering, made holy by God in the Spirit' (*Rm* 15:15–16).

Fifth and final reason: because Christians are made like that. Why does St. Paul pray? Why does he tell us all the things that we have just been reading in his letters? Because Paul knows that, for the Christian, being a son is the source of prayer. 'When the appointed time came,' – this is a creed in itself – 'God sent his Son, born of a woman, born a subject of the Law, to redeem the subjects of the Law and to enable us to be adopted as sons' (*Ga* 4:4–7).

Prayer is the speech of those who have received the Spirit of adoption. For them, talking is praying. 'And the proof that you are sons is that God has sent the Spirit of his Son into our hearts; the Spirit that cries: 'Abba, Father!' and this it is that makes you a son and no longer a slave; a son and therefore, owing to God, an heir.' If a Christian prays, to St. Paul's way of thinking, it is not merely to advance the apostolic work, but because his status as son of God finds expression in prayer; the Spirit which he has received, makes him pray.

So, with Paul and like him, let us pray for one another, pray unceasingly, pray boldly to open our mouths to proclaim the Gospel.

PRAYING WITH MARY

There are certain passages in Scripture that cannot be read without a pang of compunction. They are so true, so simple, so lovely and yet seem so remote from our experience when we read them. St. Paul's hymn to charity, for instance. When we read Chapter 13 of his *First Epistle to the Corinthians,* listing all the day-to-day characteristics of brotherly love, we cannot help blushing for our own shortcomings. A somewhat similar feeling affects the saints when they look at Mary. They express immense confidence and joy, but, underlying this, there is a sort of lament. No one has probably expressed this feeling better than St. Grignion de Montfort:

'I now turn for a moment to you, my beloved Jesus, lovingly to complain that the majority of Christians, even the very learned, even the most learned ones, do not understand that bond necessarily existing between you and your holy mother.'

This was what distressed the saint: ignorance about the bond necessarily linking Jesus and his mother. True, he says a little further on that we never know enough either about the bond between Christ and ourselves: 'If we understood the bond between Christ and us, we should better understand the bond between Jesus and his mother.'

Today, Mary's prayer and prayer to Mary are a very relevant issue, since it seems that a large part of the Church's personnel – or, as Maritain would say, 'of the Church and its personnel' – is no longer sure where it stands as regards Mary. On the one hand, we see Lourdes beating all records for cash-flow – is it tourism or something more? – and on the other, we sense that minimalism as regards Mary is almost everywhere the order of the day. People minimise: they feel a bit embarrassed about the Immaculate Conception, Mary's perpetual virginity, her motherhood, her bodily and spiritual Assumption.

All this gives point and force to Paul VI's apostolic exhortation of March 22, 1974. It is a fine document. The title is: *'For the good ordering and fostering of devotion to the Blessed Virgin Mary'*. The Pope does not hesitate to speak clearly about 'the wearing out of forms of expression and piety as concern the Virgin Mary':

'In our day, changes in behaviour, in national sensibilities, in modes of literary and artistic expression and in forms of social communication, have all influenced the ways of expressing religious feeling. Practices which previously seemed suitable for expressing the religious feeling of individuals and of Christian communities, now seem inadequate or ill-adapted, since they belong to socio-cultural patterns of the past, whereas everywhere now new forms are being sought.'

Further on, the Pope says:

'We know that veneration of the faithful for the Mother of God has assumed many forms according to circumstances of time, place, national sensibility and differing cultural traditions. It follows that the forms expressing this devotion, subject as they are to the wear and tear of centuries, very definitely need to be renewed, so that dated elements can be replaced, those that have stood the test of time can be emphasised, and doctrinal data acquired by theological reflection can be incorporated in them ... Authentic creativity must be harnessed to the careful revision of devotional exercises concerned with the Virgin.'

The Pope himself reminds us that forms of expression can wear out and that true creative activity is needed to replace them. But where has the generalised uncertainty about the Virgin Mary come from? Maybe we are now paying for having separated what Jesus said that we should not. 'What God has joined, let no man put asunder!' Now, as regards the Virgin Mary, we did sunder what God had joined together; we did isolate her in the literal sense of the word – like an island – and now we are paying for attitudes insufficiently considered in the past. We made Mary a reality in herself: she was beautiful, she was holy, she was good, she was venerable, she was helpful – and God knows that she is all these things to an infinitely greater degree than we could ever say – but we had

separated Mary from her context: Christ. True, we saw Christ
as infant or as corpse in her arms; but for many people,
theologically speaking, Mary was no longer linked to Christ.
On feast-days in her honour, as in everything that was said of
her, the bond was lacking. St. Teresa of the Child Jesus had,
on this and many another topic, a theological insight
remarkable for her times, when she said: 'Mary was more
mother than queen,' whereas Teresa's contemporaries and
associates glorified Mary as Queen more than Mary as
Mother, and thus minimised the bond between her and her
Son. What is more, in Marian devotion of the nineteenth and
early twentieth centuries, not only was Mary considered in
isolation from Christ, but Christ himself was 'sundered' from
the Father. Christ was friend, brother and food of the soul –
and once again, all this is truer than we can say – but Christ
was not sufficiently seen as entirely turned towards the
Father: Christ being essentially the image of the Father:
'Philip, who sees me, sees my Father.' We have to admit that
in all periods we are heretics, in the literal sense of the word;
heresy means doctrine separated from the total faith. In each
period of history, we separate, we ignore one aspect of the
mystery and, separating a part from the whole, we make a
'heresy'. We concentrate on one correct idea but forget that it
is related to others. Today, as we see the Holy Spirit
everywhere – and God knows that the Holy Spirit is
everywhere and more so than anyone can ever hope to express
– we must avoid falling into the absurdity of separating the
Holy Spirit from Father and Son, 'he who procedes from the
Father and Son', the living bond, the love of the Father and
the Son.

Jesus without Mary, or Mary without Jesus? Perhaps in the
past it was Mary without Jesus? But today, the tendency is to
talk about Jesus and to pass his Mother over in silence; and so
we risk ending up with a mutilated, truncated Christ, a Christ
very soon to lose his true identity. Père Bouyer says:

'History shows this, in point of fact: a Christianity no longer
willing to give Mary the homage accorded her by the Church
is a mutilated Christianity. For a while it may seem that, by
keeping Christ, it is keeping that which is essential, but this

soon proves to be an illusion. What is unique in the Mother once having been rejected, the Christ to have been retained is found to be a disfigured Christ. God and human nature no longer meet in him.'

This is what could happen today. We exalt Christ – and this is good – but a Christ without Mary, whether we wished this or not, would soon lose his humanity.

Hence, Paul VI's exhortation is an important reaffirmation of the bond between Christ and Mary. And in it we find the true, trinitarian doctrine of Mary: Mary indivisible from the Trinity, from the Father and from Christ. She is also the fairest work of the Holy Spirit, and through the Holy Spirit she is the unbreakable bond of union with the Church.

In the Virgin, all relates to Christ and depends on him. 'If you would understand the Mother,' Grignion de Montfort says, 'you must understand the Son.' For Christ, God the Father chose Mary as mother from all eternity. 'Before the world existed ... I was already in God's mind.' The words from *Proverbs* concerning Divine Wisdom are applied in the liturgy to Mary, and very rightly. Christ's Incarnation was linked from the first to the vision of, the waiting for, the presence of Mary. For Christ, God chose Mary and adorned her with the gifts of the Spirit. The same divine thought willed the Word-made-flesh and Mary. Thus Mary becomes the 'dwelling of the king', the resting-place of the Word: 'he has pitched his tent in her.' She is the tabernacle. For Mary, as for Jerusalem the Holy City, the Church uses the metaphor of tabernacle. And Mary is the Church. We are born of the dual motherhood of Mary and the Church, as Isaac of the Star said long ago, 'The one, as the other – Mary and the Church – is mother of the body of Christ, but neither without the other gives birth to the whole body.'

Among the principal remedies 'for recovering true devotion to Mary', Paul VI recommends the Biblical approach. By means of the Bible, we can rediscover Mary:

'Progress in Biblical studies, the example of Tradition, and the hidden action of the Spirit, alike encourage Christians of our day to make ever greater use of the Bible as the fundamental textbook on prayer, to draw valuable inspiration from it and to make it a source of incomparable example for themselves.'

Through the Bible, Mary will acquire 'new vigour' and a new profile.

I want to tell you about the mystery of Mary in the same way as it was explained to me. I add nothing of my own to what I myself learned from Père Rogatien Bernard, O.P., author of an excellent work now unfortunately out of print, called *Le Mystère de Marie* (The Mystery of Mary).

With Mary, we do not forge a myth, we do not exalt an idol – even if, from time to time, there have been excesses, when Mary has been separated from Christ, and Christ from the Father – but we do discover an amazing mystery: in this very young girl, the Word, the Son of God, lives not only in her soul, but physically *'in utero'*, as St. Thomas Aquinas says, who calls a spade a spade. The Virgin of the Advent: in her uterus, in her womb, is the Word of God. Nor was Christ's presence in Mary a prodigy of which she was unaware. The Angel asked her if she was willing to take part in this divine transaction, and the *Magnificat* proves her awareness of the mystery: 'Great is the Lord, my soul proclaims ... for his humble maid was not beneath his notice, and the Almighty has called me to greatness.' She knew this. She did not, of course, know all, but she agreed 'knowingly' to this wonderful motherhood. She received and she contained Christ in the name of all and before any.

With St. Thomas, I too marvel at this 'knowingly' and its four levels of meaning. First, Mary conceived Christ 'knowingly', by her faith, before conceiving him in her body. Hence, the saying of Elizabeth and of the entire tradition of the Church: 'Blessed is she who believed.' St. Augustine says:

'Mary is more blessed in conceiving faith in Christ than in conceiving the body of Christ. Her maternal relationship would have availed her nothing, had she not been happier to bear Christ in her heart than to bear him in her body.'

Secondly: Mary receives Christ knowingly, so that she can be a sure witness, so that she can witness to the true facts; and it may be thought that, in *St. Luke's Gospel*, Mary herself contributed the information about Jesus's childhood, even though

Luke reworked it in Biblical style. When we are told that
Mary kept all these memories in her heart, the emphasis is not
on herself but on Christ, whose first witness she was to be.

Thirdly: she acts knowingly, so that this may be a genuine
expression of her obedience. What Eve had destroyed by dis-
obedience, Mary restores by willing obedience: 'I am the
handmaid of the Lord.'

Fourthly: she acts knowingly, for it to be made plain that 'a
sort of spiritual marriage was being consecrated between the
Son of God and human nature.' These are the true espousals
of the Word and human nature, of the Word and each of us.
'And this,' St. Thomas says, 'is why Mary's consent, though
that of a single individual, was awaited as though it were the
consent of all humanity.'

We were full of admiration for Abraham, but Mary is the
new Abraham and infinitely greater than Abraham. Abraham
set out, not knowing where he was going, on a journey which
took him further than any known or foreseeable road could
lead. But in Mary's case, what a road and what a journey
beyond anything imaginable – unthinkable indeed, were it not
for faith! Abraham sets out on the strength of a word, on the
strength of a promise for the distant future. Mary also sets out
on the strength of a promise, but a very much stranger one:
'The Holy Spirit will come over you.' Everything that we admire in Abraham, we find to an infinitely greater degree in
Mary – for her adventure is infinitely more exalted. You may
say that both of them have faith and love so great as to
preclude any thought of themselves or of their own future.
Mary doesn't think about herself, and this is the most important aspect of her virginity: she is completely possessed by love
and by him whom she is about to receive. She is also completely possessed by faith, for, even though Mary was entirely exempt from sin by virtue of her immaculate conception, she was
not exempt from ignorance. Things were revealed to her
gradually: 'How can this come about?' 'My child, why have
you kept us looking for you for the last three days?' More than
anyone, she knew what it was to live by faith. She knew the
meaning of spiritual progress, of waiting, of preparing, of
flowering. She knew the dawn, high noon, darkness too, when

the sword of sorrow pierced her soul at the Cross.

There are two things, as simple as they are sublime, characterising the Virgin's conduct, and in these two respects she is sovereignly ours before God. Here too, if Jesus is inseparable from his Mother, so Mary is inseparable from us: 'for us men and for our salvation,' she too was created. 'She makes the purest substance of our human nature available to God,' writes Père Rogatien. The young woman, preserved from all taint for this very purpose, puts her female human-nature – and through her human-nature, all human-nature – at God's disposal. 'I am the handmaid of the Lord.' 'And she puts the Son of God made man and now her son at the disposal of humanity.' In this dual motion, in which she gives our human-nature to God through hers, and God to our human-nature, she is indeed the Ark of the Covenant: the rainbow arch uniting heaven to earth. From that moment, from the Annunciation, Mary was and is the whole Church. There was a moment when the whole Church existed in this young woman. The whole future was concentrated in her. This is not poetry, this is theology, and better than theology, it is life, our life.

When we say the word Church, which sometimes we say very badly, we must see the Virgin. At a specific moment in the history of Revelation, she is all of us and the whole Church as well. The Church is forever illuminated by her: not just the past, but in perpetuity.

It is good to read St. John of the Cross, for only three types of person talk well about Mary: poets (real poets), theologians (real theologians) and saints (whom grace makes into poets and theologians too):

Then he called an Archangel, Gabriel was his name,
and sent him to a maiden who was called Mary.
She consenting, the mystery took place,
in whom the Trinity clothed the Word in flesh.
Though the Three did the work, in one only was it done
and the Word became incarnate in Mary's womb.

He who had only a Father, henceforth had a Mother,
but a very different kind from such as men conceive!

For, from her alone, he received his flesh
and hence could call himself Son of God and Son of Man.

After the poet-saint, next the theologian-saint, Thomas
Aquinas:

'From Mary, Christ takes the flesh that he needs, from her
he takes the human nature that he wants, to assume. Into
herself, she received him who is full of all grace, of whose
fulness we live. Hence she, by then giving him to the world,
unleased on all this very fountain of grace.'

Mary humanises God. She not only gives Jesus a human
nature as general passport to life on earth, but she also gives
him all the natural attributes, all the 'human' attributes that
he needs to be a real man, i.e. a Hebrew, a Nazarene, a
Galilean, all those details mentioned in Scripture 'for him to
take human nature *in every respect*, except sin', as St. Paul puts
it. All Jesus's chromosomes he derives from Mary, and not
only his cells, but his gestures, attitudes, intonations,
everything that a child derives from its mother to constitute a
new individual.

At the same time, she affords him – though receiving from
him and being the first beneficiary – 'all the supernatural
qualities that he needs to encounter among us to make him
feel at home on earth'. So, while humanising and naturalising
God by giving him his human identity, Mary also divinises
man by offering mankind the fire which Jesus has come to
light throughout the world, and by helping him to spread it.
She incorporates us in him. Hence, Mary is the model for all
Christians and for all missionaries. A Christian, whoever he
may be, whether married or celibate, religious or layman, in
distant lands or in his own home-town, has the task of
'humanising' God; he is the individual Christ, the face of
Christ, for the people among whom he works – or ought to be.
This is not sentimental talk, but the fact of the Incarnation.

We may say that Mary's 'motherhood of grace' can be
summed up in two sentences, in these two pregnant sentences
of Père Rogatien: 'From the Annunciation onwards, Mary
belongs entirely to her child, but equally true it is that, from
the Annunciation onwards, her child belongs to everyone.'

The child whom she bears is for everyone. She bears him, but he leads her. We have to remember that Mary is the only mother in the world to have been chosen by her Son. No other son has chosen who was to be his mother! And Jesus, Christ and Lord, makes Mary the first and peerless Christian on account of that very motherhood. Even more appositely than St. Paul, Mary can say, 'For him, Jesus, Christ and Lord, I have accepted the loss of everything, and I look on everything as so much rubbish, if only I can know Christ and be given a place in him, no longer trying for perfection by my own efforts, the perfection which comes from the Law, but the perfection which comes through faith in Christ' (*Ph* 3:8–9). What St. Paul can say and do, how much better Mary can do: 'To know him' – this was how she lived – 'and the power of his resurrection, and to share his suffering by reproducing the pattern of his death, so that I may take my place in the resurrection of the dead' (*Ph* 3:10–11) – in righteousness coming from God and relying on faith. And Mary was to be the first woman to rise from the dead.

We may say that she too loved the world so much that she gave it her only Son, the Lamb of God. We can also say that she 'completed in her flesh what was lacking in Christ's sufferings for the sake of his body, the Church.' On Calvary, Mary's suffering (her *com-passio*) was added to Christ's suffering (his Passion), as she thought back over Simeon's prophecy. Claudel rightly says, 'The Cross was not the time for her to weep, but for her to learn her Christian catechism.' Jesus on the Cross, in giving Mary to John and John to Mary, was not creating the spiritual bonds which he desired to exist between his mother and us, but consecrating what had already come into existence at the Incarnation. Mary became our mother from the moment that she became mother of Emmanuel ('God with us').

As creature, Mary is the first of the redeemed. As St. Francis of Sales says: 'Jesus is the advocate of justice' by his blood and divinity; Mary with the saints is 'the advocate of grace', she pleads by the Passion of the Saviour. 'She prays, as we do, by the virtue of her Son.' And, with Mary, we have the perfect model of what God's grace can achieve in man. And here philosophy and theology can help us a great deal. When we have spent days trying by reading, praying and studying the philosophers and theologians, when we have tried to penetrate the greatness of God, greater than anything we can conceive, imagine or think about him, He, the Entirely Other and Indescribable – when we have been dazzled by God, the Source of all being, in whom we live and move and have our being, the Self-Explanatory and Explanation of all things – when we have tried to open the eyes of our faith and to expand the receptivity of our hearts and minds, when we have recited the inexhaustible and unfathomable glories of God, I say: when we have done all this and then say the five words: 'Holy Mary, Mother of God' – how even more amazing! Having seen the marvels of God, then to say: 'Holy Mary, Mother of God' Mother of Him whose glories we have been contemplating and who is greater than all that we can say about him: 'Mother of Him who is', 'of Him who is with us', who became man in Mary – how amazingly wonderful! 'He whom earth cannot contain, who made the heavens and the stars, became man in your womb, O Mary!'

In the light of this, let us consider Mary's humility – a humility as humble as discreet, for only someone humble in that fashion could receive the Absolute Light without being scorched by it and without retaining it for herself. Since Mary is entirely unselfregarding, her humility and her prayer are identical. Mary's prayer is like a flawless mirror, reflecting all the light, retaining none. The light of God entire comes into her but she, in the antique language of the litanies of the Virgin, is a 'Mirror of Holiness'. An old expression, invested with new meaning today, when you think how modern astronomers construct mirrors for telescopes. People in the Middle Ages were not thinking along these lines; for us the expression 'Mirror of Holiness' is rich in significance. To make the mirror of a telescope, weighing several tons, you have to pour the glass or some absolutely pure substance without the minutest air-bubble or anything else to flaw its absolute purity. To do this takes months, for the mirror to cool, and then years to smooth and polish it until no fault or blemish remains on the surface, to blur or distort the light of the most distant stars and galaxies. And the Blessed Virgin was, indeed *is*, this flawless mirror, a mirror distorting nothing and, receiving the splendour of the Godhead, retaining nothing for herself, giving back all, reflecting all back to God. No prayer can be more exalted than this. A mirror of this kind is prayer itself.

Mary's discretion and humility can also be verified in the history of the Church, though again they are only to be discovered gradually. In certain periods, the Church has exalted Mary, has sung her praises and built wonderful cathedrals in her honour; in others, a silence falls, as though she were forgotten; as though, passing through an adolescent phase, we were to lose our awareness of the greatness of our mother's character. Sometimes she is silently present; sometimes she is explicitly glorified. At Ephesus, she is proclaimed the Theotokos, the Mother of God, and the whole Christian world is overjoyed; and later there are Marian controversies and Mary stands once more at the foot of the Cross. Then too, there are the exaggerations of preachers and artists, and the theology of Mary's sighs and tears, masking her greatness when supposedly glorifying it, and consequently creating a reaction today in the opposite direction.

St. Bernard used to say that enough could never be said about Mary, and it is true that we can never honour her divine motherhood too much. A sixteenth century text honours the Mother of God in these words:

'She, the Lady high above heaven and earth, needs must forget all her possessions, and have so humble a heart that she feels it no shame to wash swaddling clothes or, like a servant, prepare a bath for John the Baptist in Elizabeth's bedroon. What humility! It would have been more fitting for others to have prepared a golden coach for her, drawn by four thousand horses, and before the coach to have prayed and chanted: "Lo, here comes the woman exalted above all women and above all mankind!" But no, she goes a long journey on foot, when already Mother of God. It would have been more fitting, if all the hills had danced and sung.'

(Luther) wrote this. Very fine too, if a little rhetorical. It could serve as a basis for ecumenism. There are other theologians too: (Gregory Palamas,) for instance, who wrote.

'Alone, she stands between God and the whole human race. She made God into a Son of Man and men into sons of God.' We always come back to this: the Virgin Mother is unique in being at the limits of created and uncreated nature; they who know God recognise her as the dwelling place of the Infinite. 'Holy Mary, Mother of God.' No one can come to God except by her, since only by her as intermediary, has he come to us.

a. J. p. M.

She is the cause of events anterior to herself – the long ascent of Israelite history. She is at the head of all events subsequent to her – the long history of the Church. She is a pure, receptive power with no pretention to add anything, with no characteristic other than to wait. She is our Lady of the Advent, of waiting. She is virgin and wills to remain so. She awaits everything from God, nothing from her own fertility; and she becomes the receptacle of the Holy Spirit's fertility, to produce the Word in her human flesh. Mary is not a 'specialised' saint, she is the Mother, and her sole function is to unite God and man.

Mary is the extreme point of the Incarnation. She brings us face to face with the 'to the end' of Christ's humanity. 'Jesus having loved his own who were in this world, loved them to the end.' This 'to the end' becomes apparent at the Last Supper, but had been total since the 'Be it to me according to your word!' God loved, to the extent of being born of a woman. This is the 'to the end' of Christ. When we isolate Mary, when we make her into an island, however wonderful that isle may be, we err. Mary is the most salient cape of the continent called Humanity. She is the cape, the rock, the furthest projecting point of Earth, far out in the Ocean of the Godhead. She is not an island out at sea, she is part of the continent, but she is the promontory at the most daring tip of the land, she is Land's End, reaching bravely out into the waters. That is what Mary is, and for this very reason we can always find in her the life-giving centre of our faith: we contemplate Christ in his body and in his blood, but his body and his blood come from Mary and if today he is in the Sacrament of the Altar, it is because this woman gave him this body and this blood.

Hence, the depths and riches of Dante's words:

'Virgin Mother, daughter of your Son,
humbler and higher than all other creature . . . '

PRAYING IN THE MIDDLE AGES

We have already asked St. Paul the secret of his prayer-life. And now we must ask the same question of the earliest Christians, 'who were faithful to the teaching of the Apostles, to the brotherhood, to the breaking of bread and to the prayers'. This short but very pregnant text in the *Acts of the Apostles* (2:42), describing the first Christian community in Jerusalem, was henceforth to inspire the prayer-life of Christians for generations to come.

'The teaching of the Apostles' was the Old Testament, attaining its fulfilment in the Risen Christ. 'The whole House of Israel can be certain: God has made this Jesus, whom you have crucified, both Lord and Christ' (*Ac* 2:36). On the rock of this faith and on this alone, 'the brotherhood' was built. The unanimity of hearts and the sharing of resources were not mere philanthropic acts, nor were they legal obligations. They arose from the fact that all were begotten by, were sons of, the same Father, and all were redeemed by the same precious blood. Men of faith, men of communion, 'reconciled to their brothers', the believers were then, as Jesus had said, in a position to 'bring their offerings to the altar' (*Mt* 5:23). 'The breaking of bread', the Eucharist, and the prayers of the Assembly brought faith in the living, risen Christ to white heat, as also the sense of brotherhood generated by these religious acts.

Century after century, Christians have tried to reproduce this perfect and absolute concentrate of the Gospel. Let us consider how the people of the Middle Ages used to pray. They had not invented anything themselves: the methods in use in the twelfth and thirteenth centuries, in the days of St. Francis of Assisi and St. Dominic, went back to St. Benedict in 547, or to Cassian a century earlier, and through them doubtless to the Greek Fathers. Nonetheless, even though designated by two Latin words, *Lectio Divina,* their method is still as valid today. Contemplative study of Scripture is still the great and ever-vital tradition of our monastic communities.

At the International Exhibition in Brussels in 1958, visitors were greeted with a surprise. Over the stands with their glorification of the latest feats of technology was an enormous photograph of a monk at prayer. It was nothing to do with the Vatican, it was part of the French pavilion. And a text, just as enormous, explained what this unexpected picture was all about – one of Pascal's 'Thoughts': 'All the sorrows of mankind come from one thing' – and this must be true for women as well as for men – 'their inability to keep still in one room.' The monk at prayer was the illustration of this; and he and Pascal were heirs to generations of monks, themselves imitating Mary in silence, if not in the tranquillity of her home in Nazareth. 'Mary stored up all these things, reliving them in her heart' (*Lk* 2:51).

To rediscover the secret of the kind of prayer that keeps us in our room, nothing serves better than a letter written by a twelfth century Carthusian, called Guigue, to his 'beloved brother Gervais'. The letter begins as follows: 'May the Lord be your delight!' What nice introductions to letters they had in olden days!

'One day when I was doing manual labour,' – Guigue the Carthusian was no idler – 'I began thinking about the exercise of the spiritual man. Suddenly, four spiritual steps came into my mind: reading, meditation, prayer, contemplation.'

In these few words, we thus distinguish two sorts of work in the monastic tradition: first, physical labour ('when I was doing manual labour'). But this sort of work was not restricted only to manual work; it also included vigils, fasts, austerity of life, in a word, everything that activated the body. Then came spiritual labour, of which Guigue names the components as reading, meditation, prayer and contemplation. And these he calls the 'Cloister-dwellers' Ladder', for people living the cloistered life. True, the ladder hasn't many rungs, a bare four, but, says Guigue, if we climb them in order, we shall climb very high. The 'Cloister-dwellers' Ladder' however was the ladder for the ordinary troops. For, in the monastery, there were in fact three sorts of people: prelates and abbots on the one hand, then the 'officers', i.e. those who had responsible administrative posts in the monastery, the cellarer for instance, and finally the 'cloister-dwellers' themselves. Guigue doesn't tell us anything about the first two classes. Do they too climb the ladder, or not? Have they got their own private lifts? Well, never mind. The point is that anyone at the bottom of the ladder is free to climb it if he desires to pray.

Guigue the Carthusian's 'Ladder' is like Jacob's ladder: its bottom may rest on the earth, but its top reaches far into heaven. And this is how he describes each of the steps.

You read, you concentrate: 'Reading consists in carefully studying the Scriptures with an attentive mind.'

You get all your faculties working: 'Meditation is the act of a mind greedy for knowledge and active in study under the guidance of its own reason, to discover a hidden truth.'

Then, the real riches: 'Prayer is the fervent concentration of the heart on God, to be delivered from what is evil and to obtain what is good.' 'Contemplation is the raising of the soul, ravished in God and already tasting eternal bliss.'

Naturally, Guigue qualifies all this: 'Reading, you might say, brings solid food to our mouth, meditation grinds it fine and chews it over, prayer extracts the taste from it and contemplation is the sweetness of it delighting every part of the body.'

Let us think about these four rungs for ourselves:

Reading

This is certainly more difficult for us than it was for our twelfth century Carthusian. In today's world, awash with printed matter, we reach the point when we only skim down the page. So many pieces of paper arrive at the same time that we pick one up, glance at it and, if the wastepaper basket isn't too far away, in it goes. Sometimes we say, 'I'll read that tomorrow', and put it aside, but after a few weeks there is such a pile of stuff that it goes into the wastepaper basket just the same. Whereas in Guigue's world, where each manuscript represented inconceivable wealth, reading took on the allure of a liturgical act. To understand *Lectio Divina,* we have to rediscover that liturgy; reading the Word, taking the Holy Book in our hands, is a kind of Eucharist in itself. This was how our neighbours used to behave in Brazil, illiterate men and women who wanted nothing better than to learn how to read, so that they could contemplate the Word of God with their own eyes and not merely hear it from the mouth of someone else. Thus, reading the Bible is already something important, which is not to be undertaken lightly. Reading the Word of God is in itself a liturgical act. The monks of old, who had no pocket editions of the Scriptures, used to read from a book on a lectern; reading meant being recollected and calm.

In a wonderful little book, *L'Evangile au Désert* (The Gospel in the Desert), containing a series of texts from the earliest monks to St. Bernard, a Syrian of the ninth or tenth century, called Yussef Busnaya, relates how he was in the habit of reading the New Testament: 'From dawn to the hour of Terce, apply yourself to reading the New Testament. In it you will learn our Lord's actions in his body, God's love for us and the indescribable benefits that he has conferred on us until the end of the world.'

This then is the reason for our reading: to discover and to rediscover the indescribable benefits, the marvellous deeds, of God. And Busnaya goes on – not that we should necessarily imitate him to the letter, but this is the right spirit: 'Begin by first performing ten metanies before the adorable Gospel.' That is to say, ten prostrations, bows, genuflections. 'Make a point of performing the genuflections and appropriate prayers in front of the Gospel for as long as it takes for you to recollect your thoughts from all external distraction.' – 'Shut your door', as the Lord says – not merely your bedroom door, shut the door of your heart to all outside noises.

'Earnestly ask God to enlighten the eyes of your mind and soul, so that you can grasp the virtue hidden in the words of our Lord and of the Holy Apostles. Then stand upright, take the Holy Gospel in your hands, kiss it, place it lovingly on your eyes and on your heart and as a suppliant full of fear say this: "O Christ our Lord, all unworthy as I am, behold I take you in your Holy Gospel in my impure hands. Please say words of life and consolation to me through the mouth and tongue of your Holy Gospel. Grant that I may hear them with new inward ears and that I may sing your glory with the tongue of the Spirit. Amen!" Standing upright, read three chapters in the Gospel; in the Acts read two more chapters; and in the writings of the Apostle Paul read three chapters. In the middle of each reading, perform ten metanies.'

This was how Yussef Busnaya read the Scriptures. What about us? 'Where have I put my New Testament?' we say. For the earliest Christians, 'reading the Gospel to the catachumens' was almost like administering a preliminary baptism.

Now, I am not saying that it is absolutely indispensable to perform prostrations, but I do think that there is a way in which we can effectively prepare ourselves for reading the Gospel. And the body certainly has a function to perform in this. You might say that the body warms the heart up, gets it ready. And this is important, since there is a danger today of going a very long way round, via yoga and other techniques, to arrive at what the monks of Syria knew centuries ago:

'For the monk, bowing and holding out his arms during the office, and performing prolonged genuflexions during prayer, acquires humility of spirit and abasement, warmth of heart, heat of soul, fervour of thought. Indeed, without metanies, the brother's office is coarse, cold and languid, and so are the prayers that he offers.'

How true! We think unenthusiastically: 'Please God this will soon be over!'

When Guigue the Carthusian and Yussef Busnaya prepared to read the Scriptures, they set out from a deeply spiritual, although exegetically unwarranted, interpretation of the saying in *Genesis:* 'I shall make man in my image, after my likeness' (*Gn* 1:26). For them, the purpose of Scripture was to restore the divine likeness to an image, an 'ikon', now imperfect and blurred by sin. Since God's image is not clear in us, Scripture has to bring it into focus, by a sort of photographic process. We have, as it were, to allow a new exposure, to expose the film of the heart to the light of the Word of God. You recall St. Paul's words to Timothy about people (he actually said, 'silly women' but it goes for men too) who 'are always trying to educate themselves but can never come to knowledge of the truth' (2 *Tm* 3:7). Our reading is not to 'educate' ourselves, but through the heart to 'know' the truth.

Hence, reading – *Lectio Divina* is not any old casual way of reading. This reading brings us nearer to the Word of God and so, as for Moses ('take your sandals off your feet') and all the Old Testament prophets, God requires us to step aside, to do something out of the ordinary.

Meditation

The second rung of the cloister-dwellers' ladder. There has been a great deal of development here. Think what thirteen centuries have contributed! So we shall have to take the term in its most extended sense. When monasticism began, as earlier for the Psalmist of the Old Testament ('I meditate on your Law, at night I delight in repeating it'), what did meditation consist of? It was the continuous repetition aloud, or in an undertone known as hidden or secret meditation, of a scriptural text: an incessant rumination over the Word of God. As for instance, one might say, 'I meditate on your Law, day and night it is on my lips,' or 'God, come to my aid, Lord, come quickly and help me' – over and over again. Gradually, in the course of a thousand years or more, this litany turned, according to Guigue the Carthusian's definition, into 'the methodical application of reason to a given subject'. In meditation, in fact, both elements are present: not only the weaving of thoughts round a text, but also the repeating, the chewing of the text, the tenderising of it, in a word: 'Happy are those who hear the word of God and keep it' (*Lk* 11: 28). But first, you keep the Word in your mouth and in your ears, before keeping it in your heart. And this repetition of the Word of God is something full of riches in itself. You can see how true this is, when Guigue, having read, begins to meditate on Christ's simple words: 'Happy the pure in heart.' When meditation gets to work, it doesn't remain stuck at the surface of the text but goes deep down into it, searching out the recesses, noticing for instance that 'the Lord did not say happy the pure in body but the pure in heart; it would not be much use having a pure body if the heart were not pure too.' And next, this other saying comes to Guigue's mind: 'Who has the right to climb Yahweh's mountain, who has the right to stand in his holy place? The man whose hands are clean, whose heart is pure' (*Ps* 24:3–4). Thus, meditation on the Word is not going to be my own achievement, thanks to my own remarkable ideas (though I may have some very good ones!), but primarily the effect of knowledge of the Scriptures, by which one Word is enriched by another in my heart. 'Happy the pure in heart' leads me to think about the Psalm, 'Who has the right to stand in his holy place? The man whose hands are clean, whose heart is pure.' And I then meditate on how fervently the prophet desired this purity of heart, when he said, 'O God, give me a new, unsullied heart' (*Ps* 51:10). And again, 'Had I been aware of inner guilt, my Lord would not have heard me' (*Ps* 66:18).

Prayer and Contemplation

These are the two last rungs on the cloister-dwellers' ladder. And here Guigue appears to be creating a distinction when in fact prayer and contemplation are, as far as he is concerned, one great unitary act. He now begs God from on high to give him what reading and meditation cannot of themselves achieve. 'Happy the pure in heart!' How beautiful that is! But how is one to have a pure heart? So I shall ask God to open my eyes: 'Open my understanding to the Scriptures, give me wisdom!' And with, and by, this plea, the human spirit and God begin a conversation, in which every degree of friendship will eventually be experienced:

'You see what splendid wine,' says Guigue, 'spurts from the humble grape! What a fire can be kindled by a single spark!' And he has this fine simile: 'How long this little scrap of metal, this short text, "Happy the pure in heart, for they will see God," can grow on the anvil of meditation!' Even so; meditation increases all knowledge of the Scriptures, and Guigue remarks, 'And how much longer it would grow if worked by the hand of an expert!'

At this moment of prayer, the heart thinks, 'How good, how sweet it would be to live in the house of the Lord!' And the cloister-dweller passes from gazing to calling; he has gazed at the text, he has scrutinised it with the eyes of the heart, and next, he calls, spontaneously:

'The soul concludes that it would be sweet to experience that purity which meditation has made seem so delightful. What is to be done? The soul burns with desire to possess it but finds no resources within herself by which to do so. No, neither reading nor meditation can afford her a taste of this sweetness; it has to be given from on high.'

The cloister-dweller then abases himself and falls to supplication: he calls, he pleads.

Here we must pause a moment. The urgent appeals of Yahweh's poor rise from our hearts to our lips: 'Lord, grant that I may see! Lord, grant that I may hear! Lord, I believe, please help my unbelief!' Now, we begin to emit real salvation-waves: for an act of faith is indeed a kind of wave, radiating out into the world to change hearts: our own, but those of many others too. Or it may be an act of hope: 'Your servant is sick, say that word and he will be saved!' 'Lord, evermore give me that water to drink!' 'I give you thanks for having revealed this to the little people.' But these words are always subordinated to the Mystery – not a prayer concerned with ourselves, but prayer gradually growing into contemplation of what God has already told us about his mysterious self.

This is still not contemplation however, but humble supplication animated by humility or, as the monks of olden days would say, by compunction. Guigue and his brothers drew a distinction between two kinds of humility. There was the humility which we might call reasonable, since it stems from reason: this is the humility of theologians, and none the worse for that. Please God that this humility may already be ours! It makes us understand that God is the first cause and

that all things come from him, and that I am a creature dependent on God and, more, that I am a sinner. This is the way
theological humility reasons, and very valuable it is.

And there is a second kind of humility, the kind that leads
us to supplication: loving humility, humility born of love.
'Lord, I am nothing, but you are faithful, you have loved me,
you have given yourself up for me, and so I rely on you.' And
this humility leads to 'compunction of heart'. It is as though
the heart were pierced by Christ's Passion. The first time this
word 'compunction' was used was in the *Acts of the Apostles*,
after Peter's discourses to the crowds, so there is nothing
mystagogic about it. Peter had been talking about 'this Jesus
whom you have crucified. On hearing this, they were cut to
the heart' (*Ac* 2:36–37). That is compunction: being cut to the
heart at the thought of Jesus, whom we ourselves have crucified. It is being aware of the drama in which we are caught up,
of having cost Christ his life. Understanding the human
nature of Christ and the suffering humility of Christ will kindle the fire of prayer.

A poem from the times of St. Bernard expresses this very
movingly:

> Hail, Salvation of the world!
> Hail, beloved Jesus!
> Would I might be adapted to your cross,
> you know why! Lend yourself to me,
> your red bruises, your deep wounds,
> engrave them on my heart,
> so that, loving you in every way,
> I to you may be configured!
> You, upright on your cross,
> look at me, O my Beloved!
> Draw me to you and tell me true:
> 'I heal you, everything forgive you.'
> Now, in love with you, I kiss you
> as I blush; I cling to you.
> Perhaps you do not quite know why,
> but sustain me and say nothing!
> May my boldness not offend you;

sick and soiled as I am,
may your blood, flowing all ways,
wash me, heal me and make me spotless!

In this poem, compunction comes not only from contemplation of the Crucified, but from Christ's gaze resting on the poet.

If humility effects the transition from meditation to supplication, compunction born of the Passion of Christ, leads us on from supplication to contemplation. We are shaken out of our inner torpor and slumber; we pass into the region of light. 'But, Lord, how can we know that you are accomplishing this in us? What will be the sign of your coming?' Guigue asks. The answer is: the attitude of our heart at the thought of Christ crucified, and this will imply certainty of the resurrection. Compunction does not stop short at grief over our own frailty, at fear or discouragement – remember Abraham discouraged at the time of the great sacrifice heralding the Covenant! After anxiety and waiting, come security and certainty. Contemplation is this intimate, delicious knowledge of God, which God himself gives us when we ask for it through Jesus: 'No one knows the Father except the Son and him to whom the Son wishes to reveal him.' A knowledge permeated through and through with love by no means an abstraction or form of words. And this is what Guigue calls us to:

'The soul shows how much she has been touched. By incantations such as these, she summons the Lord. And the Lord, whose gaze is ever on the righteous, and who not only listens attentively to their prayers but does not even wait until they have finished framing their requests before he answers them: the Lord, suddenly, interrupts the course of this prayer: he comes in haste, he runs to meet the soul, streaming with celestial dew . . .'

This is the Song of Songs: the Bridegroom arriving suddenly, moist with the dews of night; he comforts the anxious soul, satisfies her, refreshes her. This is 'knowledge' in the Biblical sense, loving knowledge, a rebirth with the Other. And Guigue concludes:

'Reading comes first. She is the foundation; when she has provided matter for Meditation, she entreats you to the latter.

'Meditation carefully finds out what should be desired, she digs the soul, discovers and displays the treasure but, unable to take hold of it, leads us to Prayer.

'Prayer, raising herself with all her might to the Lord, asks for the treasure desired: the sweetness of Contemplation.

'Lastly, Contemplation crowns the labours of the three foregoing works and inebriates the thirsty soul with the sweet dew of Heaven.'

The four rungs of this unique ladder are strongly joined each to other: so absolutely does each support the other that the first rungs are useless without the last two – unless we are to progress no further than reading or meditation. Similarly, we never, or hardly ever, reach the last two rungs without having passed the first two of slow and protracted rumination.

Guigue warns us against four obstacles: a sometimes inevitable necessity; action required of us in the service of our neighbour; human weakness; and, last of all, vanity, worldly vanity, i.e. preoccupation with baubles and trifles.

We too, who wish to live by the Word of God, must understand that our reading of the Scriptures must turn into meditation, and that meditation must lead on to our crying, 'Lord, come to my aid, so that I can grasp what you wish me to learn!' And that reading, meditation and prayer will lead us to the unalloyed bliss of contemplating God.

During the Middle Ages, there was also another sort of *Lectio Divina*. The one which we have just been studying, Guigue's form, presupposes that you know how to read. But there was also a *Lectio Divina* for the illiterate and uneducated. It was called the Rosary. Yes, the Rosary is the *Lectio Divina* of the very poor. I don't mean the machinegun rosary with its non-stop *Hail Mary's* repeated faster and faster. This is only a caricature of St. Dominic's rosary. The proper way of saying the Rosary – since it too is *Lectio Divina* – is the way set down by Père Lacordaire: 'There is only one book called the Gospel and the Rosary is the Gospel in condensed form.' The Rosary, the chaplet, what is it? It is the poor man's *Lectio*

Divina, in which prayer is devoted to the great mysteries of Christ inseparable from Mary his Mother. The Popes, including Paul VI, have consistently emphasised the value of the Rosary, not out of any maniacal traditionalism, but so as not to deprive the poor (and us!) of a deeply spiritual method of praying.

The Rosary is Christ: I look at Christ thoughout his life, from the great silences of the Annunciation, from the joy of the *Magnificat*, to the Crucifixion, to the Ascension, all the way to Pentecost. But this is the Christ made flesh, inseparable from his Mother, in whom he takes flesh and by whom he is accompanied, discreetly but ever present, at the great moments of his life. The Rosary with Mary leads us into the depths of the Incarnation. With its fifteen mysteries, there is plenty to meditate on there. It is a meditation, just like the monks' *Lectio Divina* – but a meditation in which the Mysteries acquire new life for us as they are enriched by our own personal experience. When I say the Mystery of the Resurrection, it is illuminated for me by my memory of one wonderfully happy Easter morning, when we made a joyful procession in honour of St. Mary Magdalen to Sainte-Baume at dawn. Hence, I never recite the Easter Mystery without re-experiencing, not the emotion, but the light of this day already lived. Similarly, Christmas: where the mystery of Bethlehem brings to mind dear Christmasses of the past. And so on, for each mystery. In this prayer, which is both recitation of the mystery and supplication, each *Hail Mary* takes on a different tone, be it joyful, sorrowful or glorious, depending on the Mystery. Not inaptly, the Rosary has been compared to a bouquet of different-coloured roses. This wondering contemplation of Christ's indivisible divine and human natures in action on earth, is within the scope of anyone, anywhere, in any condition of life.

I can tell you: when I was working on the waterfront at Marseilles as a docker, I used to pray very hard to begin with! Never having carried anything heavier than a pencil-box, I wasn't much of a hand with sacks weighing a hundredweight or more. Silently, I used to cry, 'God, come to my help, or I shall never last till six o'clock this evening. I shall be a dead man long before that!' Yes, I prayed and prayed hard, I prayed from the heart. As time went by, having carried sacks for several months, I spoke less and less, because I found I could manage on my own. One day, I realised that I wasn't praying at all. I then made it my rule to say a chaplet once in the morning and once in the afternoon. But it was difficult to take my beads out of my pocket to count the *Hail Mary's*. So I thought, 'This particular pile of sacks will be the Joyful Mysteries; in the pile are fifteen, twenty, thirty sacks, so I shall say the first mystery and meditate on that – the Annunciation; and then I shall start on the Visitation pile.' I would from time to time drop a sack or stumble; then the *Hail Mary* was interrupted by a French expletive rather than a Marian one, but the mystery remained before my eyes!

So the Rosary is the prayer of the poor. It would be criminal to take their method of prayer away from them, to replace it with goodness knows what, if anything. For here we are back with the simple Biblical method of *Shema Israel:* 'Listen, O Israel, Yahweh your God is the only Lord.' – 'You will say it when you are standing up, when you are lying down, when you are at home, when you are out and about; you will repeat it to your children' (*Dt* 6:4–7). That is what the Rosary is: the ceaseless repetition of the fifteen mightiest deeds performed by God. There is no lack of meat in this.

Yussef Busnaya tells us 'the story of a demon sent round the world to destroy Christians at the time of the persecutions':

'The demon reached a place where an old man was living, and could go no further. Having stayed there for a few days, he went back to the chief-demon, covered in confusion. The latter having taken him to task for not finishing his journey in the time allotted, the demon replied: "On my way I met an old man, whom I found singing psalms and praying, and by the strength which he derived from his God-service, he prevented me from going any further. I waited for a few days, hoping that he would pause in his God-service, so that I could then go on. But what I hoped for never happened, and so I have come back to tell you how things befell.'

By such means, we reach a continuous state of prayer in our hearts, like that of Russian pilgrims and thousands of others by many other methods. We too must practise *Lectio Divina* in its most demanding form, as also in its humbler form of the Rosary.

TERESA OF THE CHILD JESUS

The curious Alchemy of Redemption

She died on September 30, 1897, just before the dawn of our century and raises an inevitable question: why has there been so much commotion over an unknown Carmelite nun? And by no means only in right-minded circles, but in widely differing spheres. Wherever you may go, from Brazil to Japan, you will find her. Edith Piaf used to burn forests of candles in honour of St. Teresa of the Child Jesus, and when I, as an unbeliever, spent a few days with the Carthusians at Valsainte, the Carthusian father looking after the guests said as I was leaving, 'If one day you happen to come across a nineteenth century book written in a lower-middleclass style with old-fashioned pictures . . . ' and then, as though providing a kind of antidote, proceded to give a very amusing description of it, the final words being, 'Read it! Beyond the schoolgirl style, you will find a virile soul.' And that was the only book that he suggested to me. Coming across *The Story of a Soul* a few months later, I was staggered.

In the Western world's weary old age, in Christianity's debility, Teresa is 'a little witch' (Père Daniélou's word for her), bringing us back to the hidden founts of the Old Testament anawim.

Should we put ourselves to Teresa's school of prayer? She tells us how she used to fall asleep at her prayers and how often 'for lack of elevated thoughts' she could do no more than slowly repeat the Lord's Prayer. But even by this, Teresa teaches us – not to mention by her character – that prayer, rather than being a method or technique, is an open, offered life. We cannot fail to learn how to pray if we study the way she lived.

She always had one desire, from the age of four until the day she died: 'I want to be a saint, I want to be a great saint . . . I choose all.' But not the sanctity of resounding achievements and extraordinary manifestations. She wanted a hidden sanctity, in which humility would be transmuted into love, and daily life into abandonment. To achieve this, she wanted 'to vanish from her own sight' – and this is the hardest task of all! The harder we try to vanish from our own sight, the less we vanish, since we watch ourselves vanishing. But Teresa achieved this by a positive love manifested in little things. She was later to tell her novices: 'You must make your beds properly.' Yes, properly, but not more than that! 'You must make them as though they were the Holy Child's bed.' At the same time, she would reprove her novices for being too attached to what they were doing. 'You must banish yourself from your job!' 'Doing, as though not doing,' as St. Paul says.

In 1894 and 1895, she was twenty-one, then twenty-two: she was healthy, happy and energetic. She then discovered 'the secret of God'. The road she had taken was basically that of tracing God's mercy: for God seeks out the little to overwhelm them with his bounties: at this point, humility becomes confidence. The important thing ceases to be being little and becomes gazing in wonder at God's love. And gazing begets boundless confidence in Teresa. Père de Meester notes in his works that before 1895 the word 'mercy' only occurs twice in Teresa's writing and then only used in a very banal way; but from 1895 onwards, in her first manuscript, it occurs twenty times. We sense that 'mercy' was her key-word for the secret of God. Only her faith in God's mercy could justify her undertaking:

'When you asked me to tell the story of my soul,' she wrote to her sister Pauline, who was then her superior, 'it seemed to me that this would distract my heart by making me think about myself. I shall however only be doing one thing: I shall be beginning to sing what I ought to be repeating forever: 'the mercies of the Lord!'

This is the secret of not becoming self-preoccupied, the secret of being simple.

Where did Teresa discover the reality of divine mercy, if not from its Biblical source? This is more than a little surprising, when we realise what little reading matter was available to her. She did not even have a complete Bible: only the *Psalms* and the *Christian's Handbook,* which contained the New Testament. As well as these, she had two manuscript notebooks, into which her sister Céline and her cousin, before entering Carmel, had copied passages by the light of which she came to her own decision. In these, we find extracts from *Proverbs, Ecclesiastes*, the *Song of Songs,* the *Wisdom of Solomon,* the Prophets and the *Book of Revelation*. These few texts, read in faith, were to be the material of Teresa's faith and discoveries. When she says that she would have loved to know Hebrew, so that she could have read the Scriptures in the same language as Jesus did, we can guess how assiduously she studied those Biblical passages available to her. Like the saints, Teresa released and detonated the potentialities for life and grace contained in those modest texts.

'Then, opening the Holy Gospel, my eyes fell on these words: "Jesus, having gone up into the hills to pray, summoned those whom he wanted." And this is the whole mystery of my vocation, and especially the mystery of the privileges conferred on my soul by Jesus. He does not call those who are worthy to be called, but those whom he wants. "He summoned those whom he wanted." As St. Paul says in his Epistle to the Romans, "God calls whom he pleases and has mercy on whom he will have mercy. So then it does not depend on him who wills or on him who runs, but on God who has mercy." '

By the light of this, she found the answer to a question which she had long been asking: Why don't all souls receive a like degree of graces? Teresa translated her answer into a parable of springtime: it doesn't make any difference being a rose, or a violet or a daisy, 'for our Lord's love reveals itself just as much in the simplest soul offering no resistance to his grace, as in the most sublime'. And Teresa concludes by restating the purpose of her manuscript in a hymn to mercy:

'Doubtless you wonder what I am driving at, for so far I still have not related anything at all like the story of my life; but you asked me to write without constraint whatever came into my head. So my life story, properly speaking, is not what I am going to write, but my thoughts on the graces which God has deigned to grant me. I find myself at a stage in my life when I can cast my eyes back over the past. My soul has matured in the crucible of inward and outward ordeals.' Teresa had experienced the death of her father after the final painful and humiliating phases of arterio-sclerosis, and she also encountered unexpected and serious ordeals inside her Carmelite convent. 'Now, like a flower made stronger by the storm, I raise my head again and see that the words of Psalm 23 are being fulfilled in me, "The Lord is my shepherd, I lack nothing. He makes me rest in sweet and fertile meadows, he leads my soul without tiring her . . . But even when I have to go down into the valley of shadows and death, I shall fear no evil, for you will be with me, O Lord." To me, the Lord has always been compassionate and full of kindness, slow to punish and abounding in mercies. And so, Mother, gladly near you will I sing the mercies of the Lord.'

Teresa then reviewed her life by the light of this newly discovered theology; she had been practising it already, but only at this point had become aware of its structure: the opening of oneself to mercy, which overwhelms what offers no resistance. That is to say, we must await all from God, not blocking ourselves off either by our weaknesses or by our incapacities. What prevents us from experiencing the mercy of God is our being blocked off by the obstacles which we ourselves create. Here too, Teresa's absolutely spontaneous theology is an infinitely rewarding guide to prayer: weakness, misery, incapacity, without the sunshine of the love of God, spells rottenness and decay. But weakness and incapacity plus the love of God, dung plus sunshine, spells a bumper crop. We call to God; he works the transformation. Since the initiative is always God's, he has to do the transforming. All we have to do, as Teresa did, is to co-operate in someone else's actions! 'Our imperfect actions God will make productive and make perfect.'

Teresa was to go further in her understanding of the love of God, no longer emphasising her desire to love Christ, but the fact of understanding 'how much Jesus desires to be loved'. For her, henceforth, 'loving' was to mean 'letting oneself be loved'. She was not the one to be doing the loving. Loving, for Teresa, meant 'accepting his infinite love', 'not constricting the waves of infinite tenderness in him (Jesus)'.

We now come to the two peaks of Teresa's life. Six and a half lines in her *Story of a Soul* are devoted to one of them, and two and a half pages to the other – her *Act of Offering to Merciful Love*. But the *Act of Offering* has so much light thrown on it by the first passage, that the two cannot be dissociated. As ever, Teresa is reflecting on her constant desire to be holy:

'This desire might seem rash if one considers how weak and imperfect I was, and still am after seven years spent in religion. Even so, I always feel boldly confident that I shall become a great saint, for I do not count on my own merits, not having any, but hope in Him who is very Virtue, very Sanctity. He alone, accepting my feeble efforts, will raise me to him and, wrapping me in His infinite merits, will make me a saint.'

In these six lines, there are seven interlocking ideas:

1. 'weak and imperfect',
2. the desire to 'become a great saint',
3. her desire is so great as to seem rash – she insists on this,
4. she is boldly confident of reaching and becoming this,
5. she has and will have no merit of her own. Elsewhere, she says that she is 'empty-handed'. She also says, 'Even our righteous actions have their blemishes.'
6. And now the big leap forward: 'I ask you, my God, yourself to be my sanctity.' Only God can be holiness. An ingenious way of getting rid of self! 'I hope in Him who is very Sanctity.' 'I hope because I do not count on my own merits, not having any, but hope in Him who is very Virtue, very Sanctity.' She relies on the infinite treasures of Christ. Christ is her merit. This is a very ancient and at the same time very modern theology.
7. 'Christ will raise me to Him, wrapping me in His infinite merits.' She wishes to be clothed in Divine Righteousness Itself.

Now we can take her *Act of Offering to the Merciful Love of God*. She wrote this on Trinity Sunday, 1895, while she was drafting her manuscript for her sister. The title is as precisely drawn as a lawyer's conveyance: 'Offering of Myself as Sacrificial Victim to the Merciful Love of God.'

'O my God, Blessed Trinity, I desire to love you and to make you loved, and to work for the glorification of Holy Church by saving souls on earth.'

Her aim is thus centred on God and fully committed to the universal mission of the Church. 'I desire to love you.' Remember that for her this means, 'to let myself be loved'. And wholly linked to that, to work at what Jesus came into the world to do. Next follows her desire for sanctity which, according to St. Paul, is what God wants for us too: 'What God wills is your sanctification.' – 'I desire perfectly to fulfil your will and to reach that degree of glory which you have prepared for me in your Kingdom.'

So sanctity, to Teresa's way of thinking, is not something for her, but the fulfilment of God's will. And she proceeds:

'I desire to be holy, but I feel my helplessness and ask you, my God, yourself to be my holiness.'

Her desire for holiness is not self-regarding, but a response to God's love seeking an object. 'Since you have loved me to the point of giving me your only Son to be my Saviour and my spouse, the infinite treasures of his merits are mine.'

This suggests Péguy's simile: Christ's joined hands are the prow of a ship and in the wake of the Lord's Prayer all mankind is gathered. But Christ and his Body, the Virgin and Saints are all one.

'Next, I offer you all the merits of the Saints in heaven and on earth, and their acts of love. Finally, I offer you, O blessed Trinity, the love and merits of the Holy Virgin, my beloved Mother. To her I abandon my offering, praying her to present it to you. Her Son, my beloved Spouse, during his mortal life, told us, "Whatever you ask of my Father in my name, he will give it to you." '

Teresa's boldness is none other than her faith in the Word of Christ. Next follows a passage that needs some elucidation owing to her circumstances at that time:

'I cannot receive Holy Communion as often as I desire, but, Lord, are you not almighty? Stay in me as in a tabernacle; never depart from your little host.'

It was the Mother Prioress at Lisieux who decided who should receive communion and who not, and when. What seems unimaginable to us was due to the influence of Jansenism. There was, to sure, a papal decree censuring such proceedings, but the Mother Prioress, a strong-minded woman, reckoned that she knew better than anyone else what decisions to take inside her own Carmel. And the choice she made of who was to receive communion sometimes depended on very tangental circumstances, for instance, as a reward for having recovered the said Mother Prioress's rather foot-loose cat. But the Lord confected the sainthood of Teresa of the Child Jesus out of such material!

Further on we find, again linked together, her desire for God, her desire to convert, and her only resource: 'empty hands'. And this is where she shows herself to be a theologian in advance of her times.

'I want to work for your love alone, to the unique end of pleasing you, of consoling your heart and of saving souls so that they can love you eternally. In the evening of this life, I shall appear before you with empty hands, for I do not ask you, Lord, to count my works. All our righteous actions are blemished, as you see them. I therefore wish to be clothed in your own righteousness and from your love to receive the eternal possession of yourself.'

And this, God can do in an instant, as he did for Mary Magdalen: 'Much was forgiven her, because she loved much.' In an instant: 'In your eyes, time is nothing. A single day is like a thousand years. In an instant, therefore, you can prepare me to appear before you.'

Bold trust. And now come the means and the decision: for Teresa is not a woman to confine herself to pious effusions: 'So that I may live my life in an act of perfect love, I offer myself as a burnt-offering to your merciful love.'

A burnt-offering involves total deprivation of self; the victim is burnt whole, nothing remains. This is what is so extraordinary about Teresa and what comes to her from God – for in her day, in Carmel, people were more inclined to offer themselves to God's justice. This was the consummate act. One offered one's works, one offered oneself in expiation, one paid for the sins of others. In their theology of Redemption it was as though the Father implacably surveyed Christ, counting every lash of the whip to make sure that he had fully paid the whole debt of mankind. Even Bossuet lapsed into the theology of balancing the books. But not Teresa. And in this sense she belongs to the company of the anawim, of Yahweh's poor. She offers herself as a burnt-offering, but to God's merciful love, that is to say:

'Begging you ceaselessly to consume me, in my soul letting the waves of infinite tenderness overflow, which are shut up in you, and that thus I may become a martyr to your love, my God!'

For her, this was to be no legal instrument to serve for one single occasion, but a way of life incessantly renewed:

'I wish, O my Beloved, with each heart-beat of mine, to renew this offering an infinite number of times until, the shadows having vanished, I may tell you my love in eternity, face to face.'

Teresa, having pronounced this Act of Offering on June 11 with her sister Céline, for whom she had composed it, wore it next her heart thenceforth as a sign of uninterrupted clinging to God.

In October 1895, she had a great joy: she received the Abbé Bellière as her spiritual brother. Her desire for missionary expansion had come true. From the end of December 1894 to January 1896, she wrote the memorial of the 'mercies of God', her first exercise book. On April 2 or 3, 1896, she spat blood for the first time. Easter fell on April 5. And this April 5 marked the beginning of the interior ordeal as regards faith and hope, which lasted until her death. When we read what may rightly be called the 'passion of St. Teresa of the Child Jesus' – her own notes and those of the people present at her deathbed – we realise to what an incredible degree she experienced a veritable Auschwitz and Buchenwald of faith. She wrote her letter to Marie du Sacré-Coeur, the account of her life for Mother Marie de Gonzague, and on September 30 she died. Those fifteen months were the answer to and consummation of her offering. So she lived this act for one year and three months, taking a phrase from St. John of the Cross as her motto, which she transcribed as: 'Love can only be repaid by love.'

Teresa of the Child Jesus: infinite desire in infinite helplessness. As we grow older, we jettison our desires; we realise that we have been living in illusions. The illusions fade, we cut our desires down to size. Not so! We have to retain the infinite desire, in the calm certainty of absolute helplessness. The young have infinite desire, but not the awareness of helplessness. The old have the feeling of helplessness, but no longer have the infinite desire. Like Teresa, we must strive to have them both.

And this too is the essential state of mind for 'he missionary Christian. The heart must open wider and wider to the troubles of the world – which exceed what we can imagine: be it the misery of atheism or of lovelessness. But to surmount these agonies and disheartening troubles, we must count on nothing except the merciful alchemy of God. See Psalm 40, 'the curious alchemy of redemption,' as Chouraqui observes, where 'salvation emerges from ordeal and, from the filth of the dunghill, God hoists us on to the rock:

'I called and called to Yahweh, then he stooped to me and heard my cry. He pulled me from the pit of Destruction, out of the muck of the Swamp, he settled my feet on a rock and steadied my legs. He inspired me with a new song, a hymn of praise to our God. How blessed the man who puts his faith in Yahweh!'

Teresa and the Psalmist belong to the same spritual family. They pray in the same way.

ALL SAINTS
or
Humility of Heart

Let us put a general question to the saints in heaven as if we were already with them: What is the secret that they have in common? Let us ask those men and women of such widely differing periods and backgrounds how they succeeded in attaining that simple point of balance, where helplessness and boldness, weakness and holiness, inertia and grace – where, in a word, human nature and God meet and glorify each other. The saints are the very prototypes – each wonderful in his or her way – by which we learn how God and man can work together.

Though we make one of Teresa of the Child Jesus's very last utterances our point of departure: 'Yes, I have grasped what humility of heart is. I believe that I am humble,' we shall not be talking primarily about her. But she will offer the basis for our questioning of three other very different saints: Teresa of Avila, Thomas Aquinas and Francis of Sales. Without prior consultation, each of these would thoroughly endorse what the others have said about humility, and would agree that it entirely represented their common experience. And, in so doing, they will show us both how to pray and how to act, humility – the word comes from *humus,* soil – being the quality of good soil bearing fruit, as opposed to barren rock.

It was while working with her novices that Teresa of Lisieux grasped the deep and subtle connexion between humility and force and greatness of character. Forthwith, we are at the kernel of the first and most important factor: humility is neither weakness nor softness. Teresa did not care for novices who were namby-pamby (*gnan-gnan* was her word for it!). She left a fine portrait of what an apostle should be – of what we all should be, since each of us has to be an apostle to someone. The passage is well known, but it is useful to read it again in this context:

'I am well aware of being thought severe. They' – the girls whom she calls her lambs – 'may say what they please, but deep down they sense that I love them very dearly and that I would never play the hireling shepherd who, on seeing the wolf approach, deserts the flock and runs away. I am ready to give my life for them, but my affection is so pure that I do not wish them to be aware of it. Never, with the grace of Jesus, have I personally ever tried to win their hearts, having understood that my mission was to lead them to God and to make them realise that here below, you, Mother,' – she means her superior, Marie de Gonzague – 'were the visible Christ whom they were to love and respect.'

Here we see her humility in action: not attracting affection to herself, having nothing possessive about her, but leading the novices to love their monastic superior.

'I have already told you that, in teaching others, I have learnt much myself. First, I have learnt that all souls have to fight more or less the same battles, but that in other respects these souls are so diverse, that I have no difficulty in understanding what one of the Fathers used to say: "Souls differ far more than faces do." Hence, they certainly cannot all be treated in the same way.'

And she then describes humility:

'With some souls, I sense that I have to make myself little and not fear humbly to admit my own struggles and defeats; my sisters, seeing that I have the same weaknesses as they have, then admit their own faults to me and take heart from my understanding them by the light of my own experience. With others, I have observed contrariwise that, to do them any good, I have to be very firm and never modify what I have once said. To abase myself then would not be humility but weakness. God has given me grace not to be afraid of fighting: at all costs, I must do my duty. More than once I have heard novices say, "If you want something from me, you must treat me gently; you won't get anything by force." But I know too that no one is a good judge in his own cause, and next day they come and say, "Yesterday, you were right to have been stern. To begin with, it upset me very much, but afterwards I thought the matter over, and now I can see that you were quite right." '

So Teresa puts us on the right track: humility is not weakness. In Christianity, and this is characteristic of it, humility is a factor in any aspiration to greatness. It is the characteristic of the person who aspires to great things. Humility's favoured ground is Everest, not cow-hills where no worse is risked than a little tumble or two. Humility is the virtue, not of the mini-car, but of the super-powerful racer. Humility is the virtue of the *Magnificat,* for if Mary could say, 'The Lord has done great things for me,' this was because she was simultaneously aware of the humility, the littleness, of his handmaid.

Let us now question a strict theologian, a seeker not to be satisfied with words – St. Thomas Aquinas. For him too, humility is the attitude of mind brought into play when we desire to undertake great enterprises. Humility's favoured ground is also that which, in man, is source of exaltation and limitless energy: aspiration to great things, to splendid actions. Why? When we are drawn to difficult activities, this presupposes some degree of awareness of our own strength and, as we are anxious not to give way under the strain, we have to have an even greater degree of determination. This is called magnanimity. Magnanimity means greatness of soul. And this is what, if we have it, will lead us to undertake great things. Magnanimity crowned with Christian hope leads us to expect incredible achievements. When we live the magnanimous life, however, we must be careful not to lose our heads, and take care that we retain a sense of proportion as regards our great projects. And we must also keep a cool head as regards the renown that we are likely to win for ourselves. This is even more important, if I embark on some noble adventure: I risk getting ideas above myself and conceiving myself to be great, noble, high-minded.

Thus we encounter a dilemma: between our humility and our magnanimity. We are drawn to great undertakings, since we have been designed for these, and our dignity as human beings depends on them; we are responsible for our own destiny, we are called to everlasting life, we are gifted with spiritual faculties, we are capable of union with God, and it would be pitiable and contemptible to waste time on commonplace and mediocre trivialities. At this elevation, humility is born: a humble person will not ascribe his motives to anything other than what is true – for that would be the opposite of humility. Nonetheless, he will also be aware of his own nothingness.

St. Teresa of the Child Jesus used to say, 'I am nothingness, a little nothingness'. The humble man, according to St. Thomas Aquinas, sees himself as a creature; although having nothing from himself, he is nonetheless aware of aspiring to great things, be it in the Church or in the world, or as a scholar and so forth. He aspires to great things and at the same time, before God, he knows that he is in a perpetual state of receiving grace, of receiving existence and very life itself. His mind is thus lucid enough to traverse whatever is human and to set itself to whatever great thing he aspires to achieve, while remaining ever before God, beyond the inebriating effects of honour and success.

Humility is that quality in us which, active in the highest moments of our career, ensures that we do not rise above our station as creature. In actual fact, the two qualities evoke each other: the magnanimity of great works to be done, and creaturely humility (what have you got that you have not received from God?). Hence our dilemma.

In contradistinction, pride is a disordered desire for self: instead of being directed towards some great work yet aware that I am nothing, I lose my bearings and end up facing myself. The work's greatness is no longer what inspires me to action, but my own wretched, stupid, personal, little greatness instead. And this is precisely what prevents God from using me to achieve great things. What was so fine about the Virgin Mary was that she was capable of knowing that she was receiving the Word made flesh within her, and at the same time of knowing that she herself was nothing and that whatever she received was from God, just as the mirror keeps no light for itself, but returns the full splendour of the sunlight to the sun.

Père Rideau, in a recent book, has noted all those sayings of Teresa of Lisieux which could have indicated a tendency towards excess. Teresa had 'a mad ambition', she said, a desire to excel which prevented her from 'staying-put'. She wanted to be first; in a choice between the various exploits of the saints, she wanted 'to choose the lot'. 'I was born for glory,' she said. 'I feel that the Lord has destined me for great things. I have always loved the great and the beautiful.' Her ideals were coloured by those chivalrous notions entertained by the girls of her day: 'In my childhood, I dreamed of fighting on the battlefield. When I started learning French history, I was carried away by the exploits of Joan of Arc. I wanted to copy her. I felt that the Lord had destined me for great things. I was not mistaken.' Teresa of the Child Jesus wanted to be Judith of the Old Testament and Joan of Arc of Christian history all in one: 'A heart of fire, a warrior's soul,' she said.

Père Rideau also mentions another man, a little Basque knight, who too had boundless ambitions: Ignatius Loyola. From reading chivalrous romances to while away his tedious recovery from a slow-healing wound, he came to dream of noble deeds; then, reading the lives of the saints, became enkindled with a like ambition. Without renouncing greatness, he decanted and purified all that and took the way of humility, enabling him truly to accomplish his original ambition.

Puny gestures, lowered eyes, miminy-piminy attitudes of mind couldn't be further from the case. We are not miminy-piminy when we are humble. We aspire to great things. The quality of humility is, by definition, poverty of spirit, poverty of heart, the first Beatitude. You may say that all the saints pursue this and have this in common.

The patroness of Little Teresa, St. Teresa the Great of Avila, was constantly writing about it:

'Humility is like the bee, working indefatigably inside the hive; if she did not, everything would be ruined. But consider the bee: she goes out, she flies away to rob the flowers.'

For Teresa of Avila, there have to be two things: self-knowledge, the inside of the hive, and this is the aspect of our nothingness; but there is the outside too, the looking towards God:

'Consider the bee. Let the soul bent on knowing herself do the same. If she will follow my advice, she will from time to time take flight, she will come out of her inner hive, to consider the greatness and majesty of her God. There, far better than in herself, she will discover her own baseness. Believe me, we shall acquire far better virtues by clinging to the virtue of God than by sticking to our slime' – our own little patch of mud. – 'I do not know if I have made myself sufficiently clear: for, as long as we are on this earth, nothing is more useful to us than humility.

'By contemplating God's greatness, we shall discover our own baseness, by gazing at his purity, we shall see our dirtiness, by considering his humility, we shall recognise how far we are from being humble'

Thus, gazing at God and his greatness is what the humble man does most of all. By considering God, 'our intellect and will are ennobled and become more apt for any kind of good . . . ,' we leave 'the slough of our own wretchedness' and no longer stay riveted to our own patch of soil:

'This is why I tell you, we must fix our eyes on Jesus Christ our treasure, and on his saints. That is where we shall learn true humility. By this means our intellect will be ennobled, and our knowledge of ourself, of our own wretchedness, will cease to make us fearful and cringing.'

Teresa of Avila says exactly what she means to say. And when she has said it, she doesn't leave many loopholes!

This point we must insist on: Christian optimism is basically the optimism of humility. A friend of mine who died two or three years ago, a truly extraordinary man – true Christian, scholar, mystic, full of fun, very mortified – Père Pierre de Menasce, loved to say that 'we should always contemplate our true self'. What is my true self? 'My true self is what is highest in myself, however weak, however tempest-tossed.' And, like St. Teresa of Avila, he would say, 'But as soon as you start concentrating on your mediocrity and on your sinfulness, you run the risk of seeing that as your true self.' My true self is not the me of wretchedness and weakness; my true self is the me that comes from God: 'All the while we look at ourselves, we shall only see our own wretchedness and only see a tiny fraction of that. A single look at God's love for us makes us accept our wretched state and know that God wants to and can release us from it – on condition that we are willing to let him do so, and to renounce the prison of despair.' Despair at not being able to escape from this prison is a 'humility-substitute', administered very subtly by the Devil as he exploits our depressive state of mind.

As St. Paul says: 'In the light of the grace which I have received, I say this to all and each: Do not think of yourself more highly than you ought to think, but take a sober view of yourself, by whatever degree of faith God has allotted to you' (*Rm* 12:3). Humility, 'the sober view', is the daughter of faith. Psychologically, the opposite of humility is not pride or vanity, but anxiety. Teresa of Avila puts this well, in her vigorous manner:

'Believe me: when a soul is truly humble, even if God never grants her any consolations, he will give her a peace and conformity to his will which will make her happier than others with their consolations.' And she goes on: 'Sometimes, this very lively awareness of your wretchedness can be humility and virtue, and at other times it can be a very great temptation.' – She says that she has experienced this. – 'I know what this is like.' 'Humility, be it never so great' – i.e. the vision of our insignificance, – 'causes neither anxiety, nor distress, nor confusion; it brings peace, consolation and repose. Admittedly, at the sight of our wretchedness, we feel great sorrow . . . We hardly dare to plead to God for mercy. But when this humility is the real thing, the pain that we feel is permeated with such sweetness that we could wish to feel it forever. It neither troubles nor constricts the soul; on the contrary, it dilates her and makes her more apt to serve God. The other sorrow brings only trouble and disorder, it throws the soul into confusion, it is full of bitterness. By this means, the Devil tries to make us believe that we have humility and in exchange, if he can, to deprive us of our trust in God.'

If the opposite of humility is anxiety, the opposite of anxiety is peace, tranquillity. Peace is the sign and companion of humility. And here we enter the favourite domain of St. Francis of Sales. For St. Francis of Sales, 'humility must be courageous and peaceful'. Peaceful!

'Let your courage be humble and your humility courageous. And so live agreeably, and not only agreeably but happily, joyfully. When you have faults, correct them, but try to take pleasure in doing so, as lovers of field-sports prune back the trees in their parks.'

Correcting our faults should be done with pleasure, 'with gentle and peaceful humility of heart'. The humble are not upset by their falls or by their slowness to amend. Why does God permit these lapses? 'Our Lord,' says St. Francis of Sales, 'sets such store by humility that he makes it quite easy for us to fall into sin, so that holy humility may be derived therefrom.' In the old days, back in Marseilles, we used to say that there were two things which made a Christian grow – be he activist or priest: the Eucharist and 'the gas-brackets' on which you banged your head! 'Affliction must be bravely and calmly borne. Your sins and frailties should not upset you: God has seen plenty of others,' St. Francis adds.

One of Grimm's household tales, *The Little Tailor*, illustrates God's unshockable good-nature to perfection! A clever tailor contrives by some trick or other to get into Paradise. He gets in at a moment when there is no one about. The heavenly court has apparently gone out to take the air. The little tailor sees God's throne, sits down on it; he also sees the footstool on which the Lord puts his feet. How splendid! And, since he is in Paradise, he suddenly finds that he can see everything that is happening on earth. He then spots his neighbour, a poor and needy woman, in the act of stealing something or other. The little tailor is seized with righteous indignation at the sight of such a horrid thing from Paradise. He picks up the footstool (the one mentioned in Psalm 110) and throws it at the woman down on earth ... At this very moment, the heavenly court returns and God arrives with everyone else. The little tailor suddenly feels very frightened about having got into Paradise without permission and hides as well as he can behind the throne. But where has the footstool gone? Everyone starts looking for it and eventually the little tailor is spotted, trembling from head to foot. 'What are you doing here?' He explains. 'And where's the footstool gone?' The little tailor explains that, having seen his neighbour committing a grave sin, he has thrown the footstool down on her head. The angels say, 'Have you forgotten how often you charged for much more cloth than went into the clothes?' And God himself finally remarks, 'Besides, if I had to throw a footstool at everyone's head who does something silly on earth, we should soon run out of furniture in heaven!'

This is all of a piece with the wisdom of St. Francis of Sales: 'God has seen plenty of others, and his mercy does not reject wretches like us, but exerts itself in doing good.' Of course, we always have to try and combine two things: 'an extreme love for what is good' – we must try to do what we have to do and not merely allow ourselves to drift – 'but on no account be anxious, troubled or alarmed if we happen to commit a few lapses, for the first point depends on our fidelity, and the second depends on our infirmity, and the latter we can never be rid of, so long as our mortal life shall last'.

The only grave fault, the sin against the Spirit, is to refuse to recognise our weakness and to insist on calling *good* whatever particular evil we commit. This is unquestionably the worst disorder of the contemporary world: the refusal to call good and evil by their right names. Yes indeed, you might well retort that this disorder is a fairly old one, going back to the days of Adam and Eve, when our first parents thought to affix the boundary between good and evil without reference to God.

One of the fruits of true humility is gentleness to others and to ourselves. To be able to bear ourselves as we are, 'never bearing a grudge against ourselves or against our imperfections, since from this inner gentleness towards ourselves flows gentleness towards our neighbour'. Clearly, when I fly into a rage with someone else, it means that I have not been gentle to myself. I did not have the humility which should produce 'a good-natured acceptance of my neighbour and his faults'. St. Francis of Sales probably did not mean the following exegesis to be taken very literally but, of the Ten Virgins in the Gospel, he says, 'Only five of them had the oil of merciful gentleness and good-humour. Even-temper, gentleness and sweetness of heart are rarer than perfect charity and all the more desirable therefore.'

We must not confuse emptying ourselves with turning in on ourselves: there may not be a great distance between them, but humility of heart marks the frontier. In the one case, God performs it, acting in me, God is doing the pruning; in the other, my own offended dignity (offended by what?) shuts the door and sulks.

Why then and in what way is humility of heart the source of the varied and fruitful activity of the saints? The answer is simple: because humility of heart is the source of freedom, giving, as you might say, the green light for prayer and action.

Freedom first of all, because humility frees us from all the ideas we entertain with regard to ourselves: 'What will people think of me? Will they listen to me? What will they say? What will happen to me if I take on such and such a job? Suppose I fail . . .?' And not only freedom as regards the judgments passed by others on me, but even more important, from what I imagine that other people think about me, for very often we live in an imaginary world and are afraid of phantoms. This doesn't mean ignoring other people's opinions when they tell us of our limitations and weaknesses, but it does mean not bothering about what other people may think or say about us. St. Paul himself worried over what other people thought, and here was his solution. He knew that his Corinthians had been arguing about him: 'For my part, it makes no difference to me whether you, or indeed any human tribunal, find me worthy or not. I shall not even pass judgment on myself. True, my conscience does not reproach me at all, but that does not prove that I am acquitted: the Lord alone is my judge. There must be no passing of premature judgment. Leave that until the Lord comes; he will light up all that is hidden in the dark and reveal the secret intentions of men's hearts. Then will be the time for each one to have whatever praise he deserves, from God' (1 *Co* 4:3–5).

Teresa of Lisieux goes even further:

'That people regard you as being without virtue takes nothing from you and does not make you any the poorer; the others are the ones to lose their inner joy, since nothing is sweeter than to think good of one's neighbour. If people speak ill of me and if what they say is true, so much the worse for me; but if untrue, so much the worse for the person who said it, for he is the one who is going to be unhappy. It is all the worse for those who judge you unfavourably, and all to the good for you if you humble yourself before God.'

'What do you call a great spirit?' asks St. Francis of Sales. 'And what do you call a little spirit? The only great spirit is God, who is so good that he is happy to dwell in little spirits; he loves the spirits of little children and disposes of them at his will, in preference to old spirits.'

Leaving the world of the imagination leads us to the real world of action. Teresa of Avila makes a neat point here:

'Sometimes the Devil inspires us with sublime aspirations so that, leaving aside those possible ways in which we could serve the Lord, we sit back, content to have aspired to things that were impossible.'

We think up ambitious schemes, we soon see that nothing can come of them, but feel good at the thought of having thought of them; and in the meantime have neglected the small thing that we could have done, should have done, which was within our scope. 'Without my expatiating on all that you can do, I say this: Do not aim at doing good to the entire world, be satisfied with doing it to the people in whose society you live,' says St. Teresa of Avila.

According to Paul VI, this same realism was characteristic of St. Teresa of the Child Jesus. He calls it the 'paradox of hope', 'the antithesis of childishness, passivity or melancholy'.

'St. Teresa's greatness,' says the Pope, 'lay in her having been so realistically integrated into the Christian community of the times in which she was called to live. And this grace of hers seems one especially desirable for our own times. Many Christians are uncertain how, in practical terms, to reconcile personal development with the demands of religious obedience or of the common life; liberty with authority;

holiness with institutionalism; sincerity with charity; diversity of charisms with unity; daily reality with the 'prophetic' interpretation of the present. St. Teresa found herself constantly confronted with such problems. In her writings, you would not of course find these questions put in modern terms, still less would you find systematic answers to them. But no one can deny the radiance of the insight regulating her daily relationship with her sisters in religion and her integration within the narrow framework of conventual life . . . Before setting to work, she did not wait for ideal conditions or for more perfect companions; rather, we say, she helped from within to change them for the better. Humility is the open-plan for love.'

Throughout St. Paul's hymn to charity in chapter 13 of *First Corinthians*, without falsifying his intention, we can safely substitute 'humility' for 'love':

If I have all the eloquence
of men or of angels
but speak without humility
I am simply a gong booming
or a cymbal clashing . . .

If I have faith in all its fulness
to move mountains
but without humility
I am nothing at all.

Humility is always patient
and ready to be of service
she is never jealous
humility takes no pleasure in sin
but delights in the truth.

Humility is always ready
to excuse and to trust
to hope and to endure
whatever comes.

And we should also re-read St. Paul's words to the

Colossians (3:12), where he assembles all the components of humility: for here again everything coheres:

> You are God's chosen race
> his saints – he loves you
> and you should be clothed
> in sincere compassion
> in kindness and humility
> in gentleness and patience.

In the last analysis, all this is contained in one of Jesus's sayings – one, you must understand, that has conditioned the hearts of all his saints: 'Learn of me, for I am meek and humble of heart, and you will find rest for your souls.'

Thus Jesus, using the same words, applies the Beatitude of the poor to himself – the Beatitude of the meek, the merciful, the peacemakers. And this Beatitude must be ours too! Let us ask for grace to aim at great things, to be great hearts determined to alter something in world and Church, all the time in the awareness that all things come from God, and particularly leaving the celestial footstools in God's hands where they belong, instead of throwing them at our brothers' heads!

DIETRICH BONHOEFFER

Praying among Men

Prayer, like the apostolic ministry, can be a fraud if not rooted in a life simply and basically Christian. The sap common to the apostolate and to prayer is like the sap of a flower, drawn from the soil to nourish the plant. In the same way, the Christian life is a fraud if not lived while facing up to people and responsibilities – if it is only lived at the level of dilettantism and superficiality. An apostle must first of all be a Christian, even if he is the Pope himself; and this was what inspired someone to say to one of them: 'The greatest day of a Pope's life is his christening.' By the same token, a Christian life, if it is not integrated into ordinary life with its inherent limitations, is not a real one. We have to learn this lesson from men and women who have lived in this way for all the world to see, some of them indeed in the school of danger and violent death.

That is why, remembering Pascal's saying: 'The only stories worth believing are the ones whose guarantors get put to death', I should like us to look at Pastor Dietrich Bonhoeffer, at his living, his dying and his praying. I am not saying that all Bonhoeffer's ideas are necessarily the ones for us; but his life has certainly much to teach us.

The question running right through Bonhoeffer's life was this: How is one to be a Christian in the world today? How is one to keep witnessing to the presence of the Living God, present among men? How is one to play one's part in the joyful and sorrowful, agonising and serene, encounter between God and the world? For him, the question boiled down to: How should a man live before God? These are questions which we all have to ask ourselves. Dietrich Bonhoeffer's answer was differently accentuated at different stages of his life. And this is perfectly natural, given that the encounter with God is an encounter taking place amid changing events. Bonhoeffer was to die in the middle of his search, and this is important to remember, since we must not try to fit him into one preconceived pattern rather than another. We must also realise that his search took place in exceptional conditions, which are hard to distinguish from those we read of in a thriller. No one can say how his thought would ultimately have developed and crystallised.

Let us begin with the end of his life, as we are looking at the witnesses 'who get put to death'. For two years, Bonhoeffer had been in prison, arrested for having resisted Hitler. We are only a few weeks from the end of the war and the Fuehrer's suicide. Since the Allied troops were advancing at high speed, Bonhoeffer and his companions were taken out of prison; with a number of 'important prisoners', Bonhoeffer was taken by lorry from camp to camp. They all began to feel very hopeful, since it looked as if freedom was just round the corner, as the Nazis began to collapse. The guards themselves became more amenable. Then, one evening, special orders from Berlin caught up with the prisoners on their arrival at Flossenburg Camp. During the night, a form of trial was held. Here is the last glimpse of Bonhoeffer, as recorded by the Flossenburg Camp doctor:

'Between five and six o'clock in the morning of April 9, 1945, the prisoners, among whom were Admiral Canaris, General Oster, and Sack, President of the Army Council, were brought out of their cells and had the verdict read to them. Through the half-open door of a cell in one of the huts, I caught sight of Pastor Bonhoeffer on his knees, praying ardently to the Lord his God. The piety, the evident conviction of being heard, which I observed in the prayer of this deeply attractive man, moved me to the depths of my heart . . . In fifty years of medical practice, I never saw a man die so totally committing himself into the hands of God.'

An Englishman, who had earlier shared Bonhoeffer's incarceration in one of the more terrifying prisons, wrote on similar lines:

'Bonhoeffer was always perfectly calm and normal, and seemed perfectly at ease ... his soul really radiated in the gloomy despair of our prison ... Bonhoeffer was all humility and gentleness, an atmosphere of happiness seemed to emanate from him all the time, of joy at the smallest events of life, of deep gratitude for the bare fact of being still alive. There was a kind of dog-like fidelity in his eye if you were friendly to him. He was one of the rare men whom I have met, whose God was real and very near to him.'

Bonhoeffer has already been presented under so many different guises that it is a good thing to reconsider the little that we do know about his last days. The day before he died, the little group of prisoners were assembled for the move from one camp to the next. Several of them asked him to hold a morning service. Bonhoeffer did not want to offend the sensibilities of the majority, who were Catholics, and particularly of one young prisoner, who was a Russian. But the Russian was quite willing, and Bonhoeffer read and soberly expounded the text for the 1st Sunday after Easter: 'By his stripes, we are healed.'

The next day, naked under the gallows, Bonhoeffer was to kneel in prayer for the last time.

Bonhoeffer was exceptionally broad-shouldered, very big and powerful, bursting with health, with biceps which as a boy he used to flex to impress his sister Sabina; a man of great charm, full of life, a pianist, theologian, humanist, speaking several languages: a really fine specimen of humanity. A very happy childhood; a well-off family; his father was a doctor, professor of psychology and neurology. He had five brothers and sisters older than himself, a twin sister, Sabina, and a younger sister, Susanna. A decent German family: music, theatre, love of nature – everything contributed to shape these children's minds. And a great love for the annual festivals, particularly for Christmas. At Christmas, they used to read the Bible and sing chorales. A firm background of Christian ethics, even though they never attended church. Bonhoeffer's father was an agnostic, as were Bonhoeffer's brothers.

One day when Bonheoffer was seventeen, he publicly announced, in class, to everyone's amazement (in answer to the question: what do you want to be?), that he wanted to study theology, which meant to become a clergyman. He hadn't even stood up, the words just came out. Everyone else in the class stared at him. In that social environment, it was a most unusual and unfashionable choice, especially for a gifted pupil, to make. He was later to write:

'The young man savoured this brief moment intensely. Something extraordinary had just happened and he was enjoying the extraordinary moment – not without a certain sense of shame. Everyone knew now. There he was, solemnly before his God, before his class-mates; he was the centre of attention. Did he look as he could have wished? Did he look serious and determined? The thought gave him astonishing delight as he dwelled on it, picturing the majesty of his confession and the nobility of his undertaking. Not that he could not at the same time help being aware that he had faintly embarrassed the master, even though the latter was smiling kindly at him. His sense of joy grew stronger and stronger, the classroom walls faded into infinity. He was at the centre of the world, preacher and teacher of what he knew and of what he believed, and everyone was bound to listen in silence: the approval of the Eternal rested on his words and on his head. And then he felt ashamed again. For he realised his frightful vanity.

'How often he had striven to master it. But it always came creeping back and had just spoiled this moment of joy.'

Dietrich Bonhoeffer therefore read theology at the university.

Biographers of Dietrich Bonhoeffer agree in distinguishing three stages in his life: first, 'the theologian' with his sense of the Church; next, 'the Christian' converted by the Word of God. Finally, he ends as 'the contemporary' of men cast into a hell on earth.

The first stage was conditioned by a journey which he made to Rome at the age of eighteen. In Rome, the youthful Bonhoeffer discovered the Universal Church, the Church at the heart of the world. He attended his first High Mass, on Palm Sunday, in St. Peter's. 'The seminarists, the monks, white, black and yellow faces: the feeling of the universality of the Church is immensely powerful.' That evening, he went to Vespers at the Trinità del Monte. 'It has been a wonderful day. The first day I have glimpsed something of the meaning of Catholicism. This has nothing to do with romanticism, etc. I think that I have begun to grasp the notion of the Church.' The notion of the Church was never to leave him. In one of his earliest sermons, he was to say:

'The greatest evil of our times is that we do not know the meaning of "the Church", for which Christ's heart burned so passionately as he made his farewells, and of which St. Paul wrote so beautifully for us in the *Epistle to the Ephesians* . . . But it is not enough merely to understand it, what we must do is actually to become the Church ourselves. Paul calls this 'being the Body of Christ'. Paul writes to the Christian community at Corinth, to people vexed by all sorts of questions, to a community where sin is at work, as it is in us today, whose faith is weak. It was to just this sort of community that St. Paul writes: "You are the Body of Christ." He doesn't say, "You will be", but simply, "You are." This is the only thing he cares about: that they belong to the Body of Christ, whether sinners or not. "You are" – and hence these words are clearly addressed to us too.'

For Bonhoeffer, the Church was the answer to his question: 'How can one be a Christian in present day life?' For a Lutheran Protestant, this had great impact. The problem of how to be a Christian, as far as he was concerned, could only be solved in the Church. The encounter between man and God takes place within the concrete, historical community, such as it is with all its faults. And he was never tired of opposing those who would like a Church reserved for the pure and perfect, and would exclude the lukewarm, the anonymous and the indifferent.

In this connexion he said:

'An invisible Church is not what we believe in, not the Kingdom of God in a Church regarded as the assembly of Heaven's elect, but we believe that God has made his community of the empiric, concrete Church characterised by the ministry of the Word and of the Sacrament: this Church we believe, is the Body of Christ. That is to say, the presence of Christ in the world; we believe that, according to the promise, the Spirit of God acts in her.'

The young student spent a year in Barcelona, for a course of practical theology. Later he went to the United States. If in St. Peter's he experienced the impact of the Church so strongly as to condition the remainder of his life, of New York he writes:

'In New York you can hear sermons on almost any subject you care to name. Only one is never mentioned, or at any rate so very rarely that I have never managed to hear it; I mean: the Gospel of Jesus Christ, of the cross, of sin, forgiveness, death, life ... What do we find instead of the Christian message? An ethical and social idealism boasting of its faith in progress and, for some obscure reason, insisting on the right to call itself Christian. And instead of the Church as community of believing Christians, we find the Church as social institution. Anyone who has seen the weekly programme of one of the big churches in New York, with its daily, indeed almost hourly, activities: formal tea parties, lectures, concerts, charity bazaars, sports, games, bowling competitions, dances for people of all ages: anyone who has heard accounts of the efforts made to recruit a new-comer to the Church, and of the glamorous social introduction that the new recruit receives: anyone who has watched the feverish anxiety with which the pastor works up publicity and exerts pressure to acquire new members: will have a fair idea of the sort of Church this is.'

For the young theologian, already a thinker and scholar, the Church is Christ existing as a community. Such is the infra-structure of Bonhoeffer's thought and life as a Christian.

During Bonhoeffer's first term of duty, as a pastor in Berlin, he made his discovery of the Bible. The theologian, loaded with diplomas, became a Christian:

'I threw myself into my work in a very unchristian way. Ambition, frequently observed by others, made my life difficult . . .. And then something else happened, something which changed and turned the course of my life ever since: for the first time, I picked up the Bible . . .. I had often preached, I had grasped a good deal about the Church and had talked and preached about that – but I had not yet become a Christian. I know that at the time in question I was using the cause of Christ for my own advantage. I pray God that this may never happen again. I had never, or hardly ever, prayed. I was very pleased with myself, very self-confident. The Bible set me free from all that, particularly the Sermon on the Mount. Since then, everything has been different. I feel that it is so, and others round me feel it too. A huge liberation. I grasped that the life of someone serving Jesus Christ must belong to the Church and gradually became aware of what this absolute demand entails.'

His question was still the same: 'How can I lead a Christian life in the concrete world? Where is the authority dictating what this life, the only one worth living, ought to be?' The quest is the same and the answer, he discovers, is the Bible, the Word of God – and this becomes the light of his life. He writes a number of letters about this to his sister and her husband:

'First of all, I say this quite directly, I believe that the Bible alone is the answer to all our questions, and that all we have to do is to keep on humbly asking, for us to receive the answer. We must not be satisfied with reading the Bible as we would other books. We have to prepare ourselves for putting our questions. Only then will the Bible answer us. Only if we expect a difinite answer shall we get one. The reason for this is that, in the Bible, God himself speaks to us. And it is not enough to reflect on God while relying on our own strength. We have to consult him. Only if we seek him, will he answer.

'If I decide for myself where God is to be found, I shall always find a God corresponding more or less to myself, an obliging God in tune with my own nature. But if God is the one to decide where he is to be found, then this will be somewhere not instantly agreeable to my nature and not at all in harmony with me. The place which he chooses is Christ's cross. And anyone who wants to find him will have to go to the foot of the cross, as the Sermon on the Mount insists.'

He realises that he has just been fighting Jacob's battle:

'Then Jacob gathers his remaining strength, he will not let him go, he wrestles with the angel, and finally enters the Promised Land.'

And so Bonhoeffer arrived at 'simple obedience' to Christ's commandments in Scripture, simple obedience to simple faith:

'Obedience resides entirely in simple faith, and faith is only embodied in obedience. Faith has to be simple or it gives rise to reflection and not to obedience.'

Taking the Word and carrying the demands of the Word to their logical conclusion, Bonhoeffer discovered the strength of the 'pure heart', being aware of the contradictions and vacillations of his own as yet unpurified heart:

'God and the world, God and possessions, want to seize our heart and are only what they are once they have become its master . . .'

'The disciple's heart must be fixed on Christ alone. If the heart cleaves to appearances, to creatures rather than Creator, the disciple is lost.'

And he quotes a phrase which St. John of the Cross would have endorsed:

'We must travel like pilgrims, free, unencumbered, truly empty. . . . We set off, having said our good-byes, content with very little.'

Bonhoeffer's Biblical stage is his 'transcendence of God' stage. He is dazzled by God's greatness. This is his moment of 'God alone', and also his moment of 'the ceaseless and changing battle of the spirit against the flesh', as St. Paul calls it.

We are now at 1932-33. Hitler takes power. The wind of madness begins to blow in Germany. Round the altar in Madgeburg Cathedral stands a forest of swastika-banners and the preacher of the day, like many churchmen elsewhere, says:

'This has become the symbol of German hope. Who insults this symbol insults our Germany. Round the altar, these swastika-banners radiate hope: daybreak will soon be here.'

Simultaneously, in Trinity Church, Bonhoeffer was saying:

'In the Church, we have but one altar, the altar of the Most High . . . before which every creature must bow the knee. . . .

Who would have it otherwise, let him depart; he cannot be with us in the house of God. In the Church, we also have but one pulpit, from which we proclaim faith in God and no other faith, no other will, however good it be.'

Bonhoeffer's life took a new direction. Before Hitlerism had reached its most sinister phase, he told his fellow-churchmen what he felt about Hitler's coming to power. What he said struck most of his colleagues as chimerical:

'I found myself in a state of incomprehensible but radical opposition to the views held by my friends, my ideas on this topic isolating me more and more, although I was on excellent personal terms with my colleagues. I found this alarming. I felt uncertain of myself. I was afraid, owing to my conviction of always being in the right, that I might be losing my sense of proportion. Furthermore, I could see no reason for supposing that I had a clearer, more correct, view of what was happening than all the other good, conscientious clergymen who enjoyed my respect. And I decided that the best thing for me to do would be to withdraw for a while into the wilderness. In the circumstances then obtaining, it seemed more dangerous to make a fuss than to retreat into solitude.'

Finding it hard to share the preoccupations of his colleagues, Bonhoeffer exiled himself to London for two years, from 1933 to 1935. He was then called back to Germany to found the remarkable pastoral and community seminary at Finkenwalde, to train young clergy who, like Bonhoeffer, wished to be witnesses to God in a godless world. And only a Church really able to unite its clergy in the Word, in the common life and in the Lord's Supper, could do this. This was exactly what that theological college set out to do for four years, becoming a centre of resistance in the meanwhile. Bonhoeffer gave a full description of it in his fascinating little book, *Living Together* (S.C.M.). In 1939, the seminary was suppressed by the government and Bonhoeffer passed into active resistance. In 1932 he had found his vocation; in 1939 he found his destiny.

Slowly, Bonhoeffer and a few others were to become convinced that only by what many people would call treason was true love for Germany to be expressed. With the extermina-

tion of the Jews, the liquidation of the infirm, the muzzling of
the Churches, with German soldiers being poured into Russia
and dying in appalling conditions, with the innumerable
deaths due to Hitler's megalomania and incompetence, the
point had been reached when something had to be done. But
in joining the resistance, with everything that this involved,
even to becoming a member of the counter-intelligence
network run by Admiral Canaris, General Oster and others
who were all to lose their lives with Bonhoeffer later, he was
well aware of the possible consequences. In 1942, he wrote:

'Are we of any more use in the ministry? We have witnessed
many wicked actions, we have seen every type of them, we
have learnt the art of dissimulation and equivocation, our experience has made us mistrustful of our fellow-men.

'We have often deprived our neighbour of the truth, or of a
frank word which was his right to hear. Unbearable conflicts
have made us disillusioned, even cynical. Are we any more
use? Will our inner strength be great enough to resist what is
being imposed on us? Will our honesty to ourselves be ruthless
enough for us to rediscover the path of simplicity and rec-
titude?'

In those hours of blood, mud and misery, Bonhoeffer met a
girl of eighteeen – he was thirty-five – Maria von Wedemayer,
very beautiful, distinguished and courageous. In the hell of
Bonhoeffer's Germany, Maria meant something very special
to him. He fell in love. Maria returned his love almost at once.
They were happy. On January 17, 1943, they became engaged. Bonhoeffer was quite aware of the dangers surrounding
him and in which he was now involving Maria. He interpreted
his intended marriage as 'a yes to God's world':

'Jeremiah told his people at their moment of greatest
destitution that they should go and buy houses and fields in
their country as a sign of confidence in the future. This is how
it is where there is faith. May God give it us daily. I don't
mean faith that flees the world, but faith that tests it, loves it,
stays faithful to it, despite all the sufferings that the world contains for us. Our marriage will be a yes to God's world. It will
strengthen our courage to act and achieve something on earth.
I fear that Christians who have only one foot on earth may

also have only one foot in heaven.'

But on April 5, 1943, the Gestapo detected this pocket of resistance and arrested Bonhoeffer and his companions. He had only been engaged for three months – from January to April.

Now begins the last period of Bonhoeffer's life. It lasted for two years. In prison he discovered the extent to which the people with him had ceased to be Christians, or even to be religious. Sharing their misery, he came to realise that for most of them, and soon perhaps for nearly everyone, 'God is dead.'

What Bonhoeffer wrote in his last years has been so variously interpreted that we must be careful not to be too rigid in our approach. God was never dead for Bonhoeffer, but he could see that God was dead for the people round him. God no longer existed for man; man could do without him; man was alone responsible for what happened on earth, and looked to no one but himself for happiness; he believed that God was only worshipped in the olden days because people did not know how to account for the secrets of nature or how to cope with the hardships of life. Confronted by such people, worthy and talented as they were, Bonhoeffer in prison asked the same question that he had been asking all his life. 'The question to be answered,' he said, 'is: What is Christianity and who is Christ for us today? This question occupies my mind all the time.' For him, the question is not – in his own words: 'What is still acceptable for faith today?' but 'Who is he, who is Christ today for us and what should he be for these people?' 'How can Christ become the Lord of non-believers? How can one talk about God without religion, that is to say, where there is no initial acceptance of metaphysics or spirituality, etc?' In a word, how are you to talk to people for whom the language of faith and religion no longer has meaning? How do you explain to contemporary man that Jesus Christ is Lord? How do you identify yourself fully with the modern world without losing your identity as a Christian? The method which Bonhoeffer adopted and which allowed him to keep his Christian identity although cast into the world, he defined by an expression which he often used: 'the discipline of the *ar-*

canum'. Arcanum is a technical term which he borrowed from the very early Christians, who did not publicise their spiritual activities since they lived among people who did not understand them: they applied the saying of Jesus: 'Do not cast pearls before swine, or holy things to dogs.' By the discipline of the *arcanum,* Bonhoeffer for his part meant everything that has the power to deepen and sustain the Christian life in us – prayer, meditation, worship in common, sacraments, experience of the common life as known at Finkenwalde, everything in fact that contributes to fitting the Christian for a life of love lived with God and lived for his brothers. The expression also covered those Gospel truths than can and should be shared between Christians but in a different way from what could be communicated to others.

Dietrich Bonhoeffer, who was a musician, illustrated this by a simile drawn from polyphonic music. In polyphony, there is a principal melody, the *cantus firmus* or strong song, and round this the other melodies are interwoven:

'Every great love involves us in the risk of losing sight of what I should like to call the polyphony of life. Let me put it this way: God and his eternity wish to be fully loved by us; but this love must not damage or weaken an earthly love. Loving God must be a sort of *cantus firmus,* the central melody round which life's other voices sing: earthly love is one of the contrapuntal themes which, though quite independent, are related to the *cantus firmus.* When the *cantus firmus* is clear and distinct, the counterpoint can be developed as strongly as you please. The two are indivisible, yet distinct, to use the language of Chalcedon, like the human and divine natures of Christ.'

It is not difficult to see how Bonhoeffer became 'the contemporary' of his brothers, a contemporary cast into the hell of war, of concentration camps, of the extermination of millions of people. It was the collision moment with the atheist world and the Beast of the Apocalypse. We must remember that every Christian confronting a new universe is, whether he likes it or not, whatever his strength or his character, bound to endure the shock of this collision. In that apocalyptic universe how are we to rediscover the permanent presence of God? Not

ceasing to underwrite what he had discovered and experienced in the previous two stages of his life, Bonhoeffer was to say
that living as a Christian in the world, in that world, living
through the endless variety of jobs, questions, successes,
failures, experiences and perplexities: that living through all
this brings about a re-adjustment of nature and spirit which
initiates us into the 'suffering of God in Christ'.

'In us, Christ creates not a type of man but true man.
Religious activity is not what makes the Christian but his
sharing in God's suffering in the life of the world.'

By participating in the world's suffering, into which he has
been cast, the Christian becomes true man, as was said of
Jesus at the height of the Passion: 'Behold, the man!' Not to
consider our own miseries, problems, sins and sufferings as
important, but to allow ourselves to be drawn along Christ's
path and to fulfil the role of Isaiah's Suffering Servant.

Even if Bonhoeffer's thought had further to develop, we can
say that he had conclusively conquered his vanity:

'I now understand and keep on learning that we attain
belief by fully living earthly life. Once we have completely
renounced the ambition to become someone – be we saint,
converted sinner, churchman, good man, bad man, sick man,
healthy man – to live amid the welter of jobs, questions,
successes and failures – and this is what I mean by living in
the world – then we put ourselves completely into God's
hands, and what we take seriously is no longer our own sufferings but God's sufferings in the world; we keep watch with
the Christ of Gethsemane. This, in my view, is faith, is
metanoia. And this is how we become a man, a Christian. How
can success make us arrogant, or failure worry us, if in our
earthly life we are suffering the suffering of God?'

This was the last letter to be sent to his friends. What more
is there to say? Except that all of us too, in coming years, will
have to live in a secularised world, in which our *cantus firmus*,
the deep melody of our life, will have to be sufficiently strong
in God for us to be able to lead our life to the full among men.

The Roads to Freedom

A few months before Bonhoeffer's death, at the time when it was becoming impossible to continue a correspondence, he wrote the following poem, which he called 'Stations on the Road to Freedom.'

These are sorrowful rather than joyful mysteries. They are the Easter of a man experiencing Good Friday, yet seeing, or rather *living,* the Resurrection in his Passion. The freedom, the liberation, of which he speaks, is precisely that of the apostles at the service of their brothers, at the service of God.

When St. Paul, writing to the Galatians, said, 'My brothers, you were called to liberty. But be careful, or the liberty will provide you with an opening for self-indulgence. Serve one another, rather, in works of love' (5:13), he meant Christian liberty, stripping away our egoism to make us available for loving everyone. Similarly, in the *First Epistle of St. Peter,* the true context of Christian liberty is the possibility of serving God: 'Behave like free men, and never use your freedom as an excuse for wickedness. Behave as God's servants' (2:16).

Bonhoeffer's poem must be read as that of a Christian imparting his highest discovery to his brothers, and as that of a man delivering his last words.

Stations on the Road to Freedom

Discipline

If you set off in search of freedom, learn first of all to discipline your senses and your soul, so that your desires and your body do not lead you at random.
Let your spirit and flesh be chaste, entirely under control, and in docility seek the end assigned to them.
No one fathoms the mystery of freedom, except by discipline.

Action

Do and dare no matter what, provided that it is right.
Do not soar into the possible, but boldly grasp what is real.
Not in fleeting thoughts but in action alone lies freedom.

Break the cycle of anxious hesitation and confront the
tempest of events,
upheld by God's law and by faith alone;
freedom will jubilantly welcome your spirit.

Suffering

Miraculous transformation! Strong and active, now your
hands are tied. Helpless and alone, you see the end of your
actions. But you breathe and commit what is right into
stronger hands and grow calm.

For one moment you captured the joy of freedom, then
you gave it back to God for him magnificently to perfect it.

Death

Draw near, supreme feast on the road to eternal freedom,
Death, break the chains and obstructive walls
of our transitory body and blind soul
so that we can at last see
what we are not allowed to see here below.
Freedom, we have long sought you in discipline, action and
suffering.
Dying, we recognise you in God's face.

No one can experience freedom except by discipline, but
what exactly does Bonhoeffer mean by discipline? This
necessary stage and first station on the road to freedom is a
self-imposed rule of conduct. Depending on the aims of each,
the discipline will vary: the discipline of the pianist, of the
sportsman, of the craftsman, to master their respective arts,
even that of the labourer making sure that the planks or piles
of sacks are properly aligned. Hence discipline is the opposite
of carelessness: it is the serious aspect of human endeavour.

Today's crisis of faith is also a crisis in the quality of life: the
house built on the sand. Faith cannot stand on sand. It has to
be based on rock; and this hard, compact rock is discipline.
True, we shall say, as in Psalm 61, 'To the rock too high for
me, deign, O Lord, to lead me!' But we must then cling to that
rock. Bonhoeffer within himself as well as within his prison experienced the temptation 'endangering the fertility of mind
and man'. This temptation he called 'nostalgia'. Theologians

writing in Latin knew it as *Acedia,* a distaste for spiritual effort, born of sadness, resentment, bitterness. *Acedia* is the opposite of joy. Bonhoeffer described the ordeal very accurately:

'What a disastrous effect – the ruin of all intellectual fertility! There is no worse torment, and during those months I endured it many times, most acutely . . . The first effect of these periods of nostalgia was wanting to abandon the normal daily timetable and introduce an element of disorder into my life. I was sometimes tempted not to get up at six o'clock in the morning as I usually did – which would have been perfectly feasible – and to stay asleep. But until then, I had always been able to make myself get up – and not too – being sure that any capitulation on this point would have led to worse capitulations later. Purely physical, exterior discipline (gymnastics, cold baths) helps to maintain psychic discipline. In any case, nothing could be more mistaken than to try to compensate for the irreplaceable.'

The deprivations, whatever they are, have to be accepted:

'I think that it is wrong at times like these to talk about one's state of mind to strangers – for this can only demoralise you further. The right thing to do is to be as sympathetic as possible to other people's troubles.'

As Teresa of the Child Jesus used to say when she noticed novices suffering from the blues, 'Run along and do some good deeds!' 'We must never, never give way to self-pity', says Bonhoeffer.

When he says, 'Let your spirit and flesh be chaste', the essence of chastity as far as he is concerned is not the renunciation of pleasure, but the directing of one's whole life to one goal: 'It would be logically absurd to be chaste in a life not directed along these lines.' Because I run, as St. Paul says, to achieve a goal, I shall do my best to control my spirit and flesh. Chastity for a less than heroic life – what would be the point of that? 'Without chastity, there is no clear or dominant thought.'

In this battle, where the Christian is rooted in the world by every fibre of his being, like a tree stuck fast in the ground, 'the Christian is disciplined, and awareness of death and resurrection are ever before him'.

The man who has disciplined himself to freedom, can now pass on to action, very realistic action as Bonhoeffer defines it: 'Do not soar into the possible, but boldly grasp what is real.' Living in the real world, in the ordinary day-to-day, is what Bonhoeffer finds himself doing, living life under two opposing sets of influences: first, the failure of the conspiracy, resulting in his imprisonment under the threat of death; and secondly his burgeoning love for Maria and their engagement. – Two very different sets of circumstances, which he intends to live out 'in reality'.

He discusses the failure with his brother-in-law, Hans von Donhanyi, who master-minded the plot; Hans had in a sense got Dietrich into prison, and Hans, also in prison, then wrote to him: 'Forgive me. I have got you into a terrible mess.' Bonhoeffer replied:

'You must realise that my spirit is without the slightest atom of reproach or bitterness as regards what has befallen us, you and me. Such things come from God and from him alone. And I know that we are united, you, Christel (Dietrich's sister) and I, in the conviction that, before God, the only things are submission, perseverance, patience – and gratitude. This rules out any question of 'Why?' No, you must not feel sorry about us. Someone Else has already absolved you.'

And about his engagement, he wrote in the same letter:

'I have to tell you – so that you can share my happiness – that since January I have been engaged to Maria. I am certain that this experience is good for both of us, although for the time being it may be hard to understand.'

Bonhoeffer then quoted a hymn, which he used to repeat as a prayer in prison: 'Joy and suffering come at night but leave without your knowing, to report how you have borne them to the Lord.'

You remember that he wrote to his fiancée that, like Jeremiah, their marriage would be 'a yes to God's world':

'We must find God, and love him through what he gives us in the here-now. If he is pleased to lavish earthly happiness on us, we must not be more pious than he is and spoil this happiness by presumptuous or provoking thoughts, or by an excessive religious imagination never content with what he gives us.'

Give thanks to the Lord, accept what comes from him: as Pascal says, 'All things are like masters coming from the hand of God. We must learn to obey them.'

If Bonhoeffer in his prison experienced a nostalgia which could only be cured by strict discipline, he also found that action presented an analogous temptation: desires for the future. Pseudo-action, not real action, since it does not act in time present, but nourishes itself on dreams. His imagination was powerfully tempted when bird-song reached him in his cell:

'I am sitting in my cell on the top floor; in the house everything is quiet; a few birds are still singing and I can even hear a cuckoo calling in the distance. These long warm summers – this is the second one I have spent here – weigh me down. I long to get out, and might do silly things.'

So what is to be done? Repress all his yearnings? And risk blowing up?

'You see, this evening I wouldn't dare to imagine myself as sitting with Maria and you in your garden, by the water, talking until darkness falls. This would merely be torturing myself and doing myself physical harm. That is why I take refuge in thinking, in letter-writing and keep my desires at a distance out of self-protection.'

Bonhoeffer knew his own weakness, he felt that a man should not cling to his desires. For him, freedom lay not in 'fleeting thoughts,' but in action. The freest man is the one who acquires the greatest mastery, not of the universe, but of his choices, the one who sets himself freest inside: 'Break the cycle of anxious hesitation and confront the tempest of events.'

Suffering too is on the road to freedom, but only if it is prized, and highly prized. When the ground gives way beneath our feet, when there is nothing but distress and tribulation. St. Paul says, 'We can boast about our sufferings. These sufferings bring patience, as we know, and patience brings perseverance, and perseverance brings hope; and this hope is not deceptive' (*Rm* 5:3–5).

For Bonhoeffer, suffering was that high, dangerous and very necessary action in which he had been taking part and which

had now collapsed. Without repining over what might have
been, though not minimising the need for and the importance
of what he had undertaken, Bonhoeffer committed his action
into God's hands, as the Psalmist and Jesus committed their
souls into the Father's hands. Bonhoeffer was sure that God
would magnificently perfect his action:

> You commit what is right
> into stronger hands and grow calm.
> For one moment you captured the joy of freedom,
> then you gave it back to God.

And thus he uncovers the true difference between
Christians and pagans, which he expresses in another poem
written at the same time:

> Men go to God in all their misery
> and ask for help, happiness and bread,
> ask to be saved from illness, sin and death,
> all do this, all, Christians and pagans.

> Some men go to God in his misery,
> find him poor, despised without shelter or bread,
> see him overwhelmed by sin, weakness and death,
> Christians are with God in his Passion.

> God goes to all men in their misery,
> God feeds their body and soul with his bread,
> for Christians and pagans God suffers death on the cross
> and his forgiveness is for all, Christians and pagans.

To God, Bonhoeffer commits all that he himself can no
longer do, but the God whom he encounters is Jesus at
Gethsemane: the God of the passion, he 'who lays down his
life'.

In the last analysis, freedom for Bonhoeffer comes from concentrating on the essential. As well as in discipline, in action,
in suffering as in death, freedom results from contemplation of
the Uniquely Necessary. He produced this extraordinary formula – found later on a scrap of paper: 'What is freedom? –

'Love of freedom in prison.'

No one could take this freedom from him, since it was completely interior. In one of the last things he wrote: *Freedom and Obedience,* he summed up his thinking of the moment, and summed up his whole life as well:

'Jesus stands before God as he who obeys in freedom. In obedience, he performs the Father's will, by observing the law laid on him to the letter. In freedom, he says, "Yes," to the divine will, in a completely personal decision, with open eyes and joyful heart. It is as though he re-created that will as his own. Obedience without freedom is slavery. Freedom without obedience is arbitrary. Obedience binds freedom, and the latter ennobles obedience. Obedience binds the creature to his Creator, freedom sets him face to face with Him who has created him in His own image.'

Though Dietrich Bonhoeffer's thought remained incomplete, his life ended with him being present to men and being present to God, freely, obediently, although at the price of the four stations, discipline, action, suffering and death, each of them being prelude to resurrection.

So what did prayer mean for Bonhoeffer?

'Preparing myself to receive the Word as a personal message in the tasks that are mine, in my decisions, in my sins and in my temptations.'

What Dietrich Bonhoeffer taught to the future pastors of Finkenwalde, he himself put into practice.

WALKING IN GOD'S PRESENCE

I should like to conclude what I have been saying about prayer as taught by the Masters, by recommending one attitude of mind. Perhaps some of us will react to it like Naaman the Syrian, refusing to dive into the Jordan because it seemed so small in comparison with the rivers of his native land: for leprosy, that was too simple a cure! But we must grasp the point that, with God, only very simple means – which doesn't mean either simplistic or always easy ones – can put us on the right road to meeting him.

To illustrate this, let us once again listen to the Word of God in that famous Old Testament passage describing Elijah's encounter with God at Horeb. Discouraged by the attacks of Yahweh's enemies and by his own weakness ('I am no better than my forefathers'), he fled and, miraculously sustained by food which he found when he woke up, walked through the wilderness for forty days and forty nights until he reached the Mountain of God: Sinai (here called Horeb), that same place where God had revealed his Name in the Burning Bush and given his law to Moses. Elijah had thus returned to the source of his ancestral faith, advancing to meet his God. The long journey is worth a comment: forty days, reminiscent of the forty years of the Exodus, and anticipating Christ's forty days of temptation. You do not make an appointment with God to meet him at such and such a time and place, but you journey to meet him, humbly and patiently. And God mysteriously sustains us on our journey, even when we don't see how.

'Having reached Horeb, Elijah was told: "Come out, and stand on the mountain before Yahweh." And God passed by. There was a hurricane so strong that it tore the mountains and shattered the rocks at Yahweh's approach, but Yahweh was not in the hurricane; and after the hurricane, an earthquake, but Yahweh was not in the earthquake; and after the earthquake, a fire, but Yahweh was not in the fire; and after the fire, the sound of a gentle breeze, a gentle murmur. As soon as Elijah heard this, he covered his face with his cloak and went out and stood at the entrance to the cave. Then a voice came to him' (1 *K* 19:11–14). In this passage, as the note in the *Jerusalem Bible* says, 'the murmur of a gentle breeze' symbolises the spiritual nature of God and the intimacy of his dealings with his prophet: but be warned! There is also the hurricane, the wind, the storm, the earthquake, symbolic of the terrible commands that the prophet will be given. God may speak in a murmur, but his actions are not gentle, and frequently they are terrifying. He is the consuming fire.

There is a fine sentence in an old spiritual writer called Duguet, which might have been intended as a commentary on Elijah:

'As only God should be listened to, he speaks low, exactly as he pleases. The least sound stifles his voice.'

This doesn't mean external noises – which are sometimes unavoidable – but the uproar which we could control if we tried, particularly the commotion inside ourselves.

Concerning the encounter with God, we shall consider three things. First of all, the real and abiding actuality of God's presence, which the Bible calls the gaze or face of God. Then, the no less fundamental attitude that this reality entails on our part: continually to seek God's presence: 'You must pray continually,' Jesus says (*Lk* 18:1). And finally, we shall try to see the humble means for this encounter.

The ever-present face of God

First then, the continual omni-presence of God. This presence is the common treasure of mankind, so pithily expressed in the Arabic proverb: 'A black ant on a black stone on a dark night: God sees it.' This is the most ecumenical, the most universal truth of all religions and of all those major philosophies still preserving a sense of powers transcending man's. It was also the common heritage of the antediluvian partriarchs described in the early chapters of *Genesis*.

'Walking in the presence of God' are words used in the Bible to characterise two men who lived before the Flood, two righteous men among corrupt mankind. They were no part of the people of Israel, for the latter did not then as yet exist, but Jewish tradition considered Enoch and Noah as two of God's friends, two Old Testament saints: 'pagan saints' the late Père Daniélou called them.

To Enoch, the Bible accords a special place: he is the seventh person to be mentioned after Adam (*Gn* 5:23). Seven, is a special number, the perfect number, and the length of Enoch's life is not accidentally set at 365 years: this representing a year of years, as many years as there are days in the solar year. More important than this, however, *Genesis* says with telling brevity: 'Enoch walked with God,' which means that he lived on friendly terms with God, was admitted to the secret of God. Then 'he disappeared, because God took him.' Enoch plays an important part in Jewish tradition; not only was his story embellished with legends, but the author of the *Epistle to the Hebrews* refers to him when speaking about the Ancestors bearing witness to God by faith: 'Enoch had pleased God. Now, it is impossible to please God without faith, since anyone who comes to him must believe that he exists and that he rewards those who try to find him' (*Heb* 11:5–6).

The same thing is said of Noah: 'Noah was a good man, a man of integrity among his contemporaries, and he walked with God' (*Gn* 6:9). He too lived on friendly terms with God. And so we come to Abraham: Yahweh appeared to him and said, 'I am El Shaddai. Walk in my presence and be perfect' (*Gn* 17:1). It is the same for Abraham as for Enoch and Noah. Has the friendship with God of those primeval days diminished since? They 'walked with God' as you might walk along the road with a friend. Abraham 'walked in God's presence.' Possibly the expression contains an element of greater distance than we can tell, but the fact is there, clear enough.

What about us? Are we too supposed to join the walk with God? Yes, for Zechariah's prophecy in the *Benedictus* has to be fulfilled in us, and so does the 'holy covenant, the oath sworn to Abraham by the terms of which we are enabled to serve God in holiness and righteousness before him, all the days of our life' (*Lk* 1:72–75). Strong and sure is the faith of the Baptist's father, bringing the promise true for his own generation and for ours, though made to his ancestor Abraham, eighteen hundred years before.

Eighteen hundred years – but not eighteen hundred years of silence. Like a hinge between the patriarchs and Zechariah, we have the wonderful passage in Micah on Yahweh's lawsuit with Israel:

'Now, listen to what Yahweh is saying:

"Stand up! and let the case begin before the mountains, and let the hills hear what you say! Listen, you mountains, to Yahweh's accusation." '

Yahweh puts his people on trial, and the people reply:

"With what shall I come into Yahweh's presence? Shall I bow to the ground? Shall I come with holocausts? Must I offer my first-born to pay for my sin?"

Then God's answer cuts through the rhetoric like a laser-beam:

"You have already been told, O man, what is right, what Yahweh requires of you: only this – to do what is right, to love tenderly and to walk humbly with your God."

Again we have this walking in God's presence: literally we should translate: 'and to make your walk humble with your God'.

Since God's presence is the abiding treasure of our human nature, we must pause over this a little longer. The Psalms linger over this again and again. When we seek God's grace, he for his part is looking at us. 'Yahweh looks down from heaven, he sees the whole human race' (33:13). 'Mark this, Yahweh watches over those who fear him, who rely on his love to rescue them from Death' (33:18). This is the great truth. God is always looking at us. A child knows this; but when this becomes real to us in adult life, how our whole outlook changes! 'Protect me, O God, I have taken refuge in you!' (*Ps* 16:1). God's blessing is none other than his gaze. 'This is how you are to bless the children of Israel. You will say: "May

Yahweh bless you and keep you! May Yahweh let his face shine on you and be gracious to you! May Yahweh uncover his face to you and bring you peace!" ' (*Dt* 6:23–27).

God's gaze forever resting on us generates his presence in its immensity and in its intimacy. This is what we might call the cosmic presence of God. We should reflect on this mystery; it is the mystery of existence. I am not talking Aristotle or St. Thomas Aquinas now. I mean our very lives. The universe depends on God day and night, second by second. A candle-flame or the remotest galaxy alike would not exist, if God did not preserve, did not keep them in existence. This has nothing to do with philosophy: this is the essential fact of the cosmos, the primal truth. And such a simple one! This was how it was discovered by a lad who told me about it himself. He had grown up amid every possible and imaginable hardship – one of those children and adolescents who pass through the hands of every variety of social worker and specialised teacher. Eventually, he ended up in the French equivalent of a Borstal. There he was: lonely, without religion, and without culture. Bored, one day, he was looking at his ball-point pen, when he thought: 'This is new. One day it will be worn out.' Then, looking at a house that was going up, he thought: 'This house is new; one day, it will be old and tumble down.' Although he had never opened a book in his life, the thought then came to him: 'But is there anything in the world that doesn't get old?' He had stumbled on the question central to all philosophy.

Is there a being in the world that doesn't get old? This very intelligent ignoramus had stumbled on the mystery of the cosmos. We are only contingent beings, as philosophers say, i.e. beings that might not have been. We are not indispensable in ourselves. None of us is indispensable, 'necessary' as the philosophers put it. If I were indispensable, i.e. 'necessary', I should always have existed and always should exist. But as I have not always existed and as I shall not always exist, I am not an indispensable being, nor were my parents, nor anything else in the world, nor the world itself. They could all not have existed.

But a being that is not indispensable and yet exists must depend on a being which in fact is indispensable. How are we to understand that? That at every second the relative and totally dependent being that I am – I am not merely talking about my life, but about my essential self – the un-necessary being that I am needs a being which is indispensable. Here is a simile to give us some idea (not a demonstration, however): think of thousands of millions of mirrors reflecting light; they reflect the light from one to the next, but there has to be an initial source of light, for the mirrors do not generate light but merely receive it. Without an initial light to transmit from one to the next, there would be darkness. The mirrors are only receivers and transmitters: they are only light by participation. Similarly with existence: we receive body and existence, but we are not body and existence. And this was what the lad was looking for: a being who not only could not grow old but whose existence would be self-defining, who could not not exist.

God would be diminished and mutilated in us, were the difference between him and us not so obvious. God alone exists. God alone cannot not be. And everything existing outside God is called into existence by him out of nothingness. He *is* existence; whereas I *have* existence, I receive it. This is something perfectly simple, but it needs to be thought about: we must realise that we are not indispensable, and that God alone has conjured us out of nothing. My frailty is something of value then: I exist, although nothing in me summoned me into existence. The day when this becomes our light (and not a philosophic problem), a constant relationship is established between God and us; God's tenderness becomes clear to us. If I now exist, if I am present now, if I last a little longer, this is because God is sustaining me now, minute by minute, in existence. There is, as it were, a umbilical cord linking me to God. My watch, this paper, that bird-song, everything, lasting or fleeting, only exists because God endows it with his own being. Psalm 104 expresses this very clearly, and more simply than I can, but what I have been saying will make you appreciate it all the more:

'Turn your face away and they expire' – all creatures – 'take back your spirit and they die

and revert to their clay;
send out your spirit, they are made anew,
and you restock the surface of the earth.'

Such is the presence of existence, the immensity of God, of
which I find myself to be a part; 'In him, we have life, movement and being,' St. Paul says (*Ac* 17:28). Can a flower forget
the stalk supporting it and giving it existence minute by
minute? I am a permanent crumb of the indestructible bread
of God, or to put it in a phrase quoted by Maritain, 'I am of no
importance to the world but not of no importance before God.'
For this reason and only for this reason, I am the most important person for myself. If I am here, I am one of God's
thoughts. The father of the prodigal son waited for him to
come home but could do nothing in the meanwhile; God, for
his part, continuously begets me into existence in respect of
every particle of my being.

From this wonderful thought of the existence and immensity of God springs a second, related thought: the presence of
grace. God brings me into intimacy with him. God, by bringing me into existence, makes me a son with the Son. I am able
to say 'Our Father'. I become a dwelling of the Holy Spirit.

The saints and mystics have never divorced, much less opposed, these two presences: they have always linked the
presence of grace to the presence of the immensity of God.
Whether we are thinking of St. Teresa of Avila, St. John of the
Cross, St. Francis of Sales or St. Francis of Assisi, or anyone
else you care to name, 'we always find the same theme being
strongly stressed: God is present in the inner self of every
creature, and hence we find him when we look into ourselves'
(Cognet).

The two presences of God, the one beginning with what is
most tangible in the world, and the other culminating in the
presense of the Trinity within us, produce a great calm.

Every saint expresses this in his own way. St. Paul says: 'We
know that, by turning everything to their good, God
co-operates with all those who love him, and with all those
whom he has called in accordance with his purpose' (*Rm*
8:28).

'O ever-tranquil Trinity, tranquil God who calmest all!' says a medieval Latin poem. The Psalmist's 'I take refuge in your hand' is even truer for us than for a bird cowering in a man's hand, since the most inward aspect of our existence is already in God's hand. And so, we can really be, as St. Elizabeth of the Trinity said, 'as still and peaceful as if we were already in eternity'. In faith, I rejoin God who is present, here. And even when there are storms and set-backs, when I am fed up or down on my luck, I am calm: I cannot doubt the existence of God since I exist and God keeps me in his gaze. My strength will lie in seeking the face of God. 'Come, said my soul, seek his face! O Yahweh, your face will I seek!' (*Ps* 27:8).

'How soon shall I drink deep of the presence of God?' (*Ps* 42:2). 'Seek out Yahweh, seek his strength, seek out his perpetual presence!' (*Ps* 105:4).

In this quest, I am helped twice over, God always being the first to take the initiative; his gaze precedes my gaze and I am drawn into the orbit of God's face, as though invisibly caught in that orbit. The Moslem saint and mystic Al-Hallaj puts this sublimely: 'I call you – no, you call me to you. How could I have spoken to you, had you not spoken to me?' When we sing, 'Yahweh, your face will I seek', we could sing – and it would be even truer: 'You seek your image, Lord, down in the depths of my heart' – for God seeks his own image, his image and likeness, in us.

But there is another road, an infinitely direct one: we find the face of God in the face of Christ. Just as the presence of grace grafted on to the presence of being, leads us to intimacy with God, so the face of God dominating the Old Testament appears to us now, when we look at Christ: 'He who sees me, sees the Father,' Jesus said to Philip (*Jn* 14:9). Henceforth we have to seek 'the knowledge of God's glory radiant in the face of Christ' (2 *Co* 4:6). Yes, God's glory shines forth from the face of Christ, for, as St. John tells us: 'No one has ever seen God; the only Son, who is nearest the Father's heart, is the one who has made him known' (*Jn* 1:18). He is 'the radiant light of God's glory and the perfect copy of his nature, the Son, sustaining the universe by his powerful command' (*Heb* 1:3). And we are ourselves transformed by this glory: 'And we, with

our faces unveiled, like mirrors reflecting the brightness of the
Lord, all grow brighter and brighter until we are turned into
the image that we reflect; this is the work of the Lord, who is
Spirit' (2 *Co* 3:18). This is what eternal life will be: 'They will
see his face, and his Name will be written on their foreheads'
(*Rv* 22:4).

St. John of the Cross knew all about the mystery of the
transforming gaze:

> When you were looking at me,
> your eyes conveyed your grace into me;
> this was because you loved me,
> and my eyes, seeking your image,
> have the right to adore what they found in you.
>
> Do not spurn me,
> for if you originally saw black in me,
> you may now look at me,
> having already looked at me
> and bestowed grace and beauty on me.

Humble means for the encounter

These divine truths are not beyond our reach; very humble
means – think of Naaman the leper! – allow us to walk in the
presence of God. The first is what the Carthusians, in the true
Benedictine tradition, call 'turning to God'. Nothing could be
simpler. I look at God, who is looking at me. Looking at God
is good, but how much better when I look at God when he is
actually looking at me! It is not just me trying to say
something to God, but me contemplating God who himself is
looking at me. Like the young mother, pushing the baby in the
pram, you see that ecstatic look, the young mother's smile,
whether the baby is asleep or looking back at her. No woman
is not transfigured by such a smile. But when it is God, and I
capture his smile! My gaze intercepts God's gaze and, as in a
mirror, I receive God's gaze fixed on me. From that meeting of
eyes, a loving union is born and, as a result, I shall correct

whatever does not conform to God in me. If I walk past a mirror, I straighten my tie. Similarly, when I look at God looking at me, I straighten my soul's tie!

But what am I to do to remind myself to look at God looking at me? If we truly want to do this, we must, each in our own way, do what the author of the *Book of Numbers* commands by the voice of Moses: put a purple thread in the fringe of our shawl or of our cloak, so that when we see the purple thread we recall all Yahweh's commands, 'to put them into practice' and to be 'consecrated for God', The purple-threaded fringe recalled the sacred character of the community created by God: a people of priests – we often sing this without thinking what it means! Man is inconstant and must humbly accept these reminders, otherwise 'he follows the desires of his heart and of his eyes!' So, when we, for our part, shut such and such a door, or go up such and such a flight of stairs, we may use this as a reminder, as an occasion for 'turning to God'. The monks have a bell which they ring; but for us, a factory siren, a passing jet, can equally well make us 'look at God who is looking at us'. This isn't very natural, you may object. Nothing is too little, if the objective is grand enough; and here the objective is God himself. So, whatever our own timetables, rhythms and means of transport may be – for instance, when pressing the button for the lift, or when turning on the electric cooker – we can 'turn to God'. – and life and kitchen will be transformed. If we have faith, we must believe this. The saints do not think up complicated methods. They believe in simple, humble things. And because the things are simple, they then apply themselves to doing them.

A variant of 'turning to God' is the prayer of the heart, in which we constantly hold the name of Jesus: 'Whoever calls on the name of the Lord will be saved' (*Ac* 2:21). The prayer of the heart is the great prayer of Eastern tradition: 'Lord Jesus, Son of the Living God, have pity on me!' This is the cry of the blind man of Jericho (*Lk* 18:38). The prayer of the tax-collector: 'God, be merciful to me, a sinner!' (*Lk* 18:13). Repeating this 'throughout our days' is what Eastern monks call 'breathing the name of Jesus'. You breathe the name of Jesus as though it were the perfume of the *Song of Songs*, wafted abroad and inhaled with delight. Breathing the name of Jesus can become the very 'breathing of the heart'. Yes, in a physical sense, if we make the prayer coincide with our own breathing-rhythm: 'Lord Jesus, Son of the Living God, be merciful to me, a sinner!'

But nothing, no method, no special grace, nothing can replace humility of heart. All these things, prayers on waking up, Name of Jesus and so forth, only have value by virtue of the humility of heart which they express. Here is the advice of an Eastern monk called Silwan, born in Russia in 1866, monk of Mount Athos in 1892, died in 1938. He is thus almost our contemporary. He was a peasant, he seduced a girl, killed a man, then became a monk. People didn't want to know about him in his own country, so he left and went to Mount Athos. Silwan wrote as follows:

'If you want to pray in your heart and you are not capable of doing so, be content with saying the prayer with your lips, and keep your spirit attentive to what you are saying. Gradually, the Lord will give you the grace of interior prayer as well, and then you will be able to pray without distraction. Do not try to achieve the prayer of the heart by technical means; you will damage your heart and, in the end, still only pray with your lips.'

Our prayer must well up from the depths of God's presence.

'Grasp the order of the spiritual life: God grants his gifts to the humble, sincere soul. Be obedient, be moderate in all things, in food, in speech, in everything you do; and then the Lord himself will give you the grace of interior prayer.'

And Silwan goes on:

'The soul of a humble man is like the sea: if you throw a stone into the sea, the surface of the water is momentarily disturbed; then the stone sinks into the depths. Thus, all suffering is swallowed up in the heart of the humble man, since the strength of God is in him.'

For humility of heart also entails a loving acceptance of events. That was what Père de Caussade used to teach: 'Each moment brings a duty which we must faithfully discharge.' He was fond of using the simile of the clock-hand, each minute covering the space allotted, never worrying about the space to come, nor about the space just gone. This is Mary's very simple answer: 'Be it to me according to your word.'

This faithfulness to the will of God is to be observed even in the most trivial things. 'The power of the Most High will cover you with his shadow,' but the shadow is the often dark and confusing form in which the presence of God appears (or hides). It may be something that looks like a shadow; the visible aspect may seem to be what occurs to everyone, everyday; but the invisible, clung to by faith, is the presence of God, God present. Madeleine Delbrêl knew all about this, as woman, as poet and as daughter of God:

'I do not mean learning to dally. We must learn to be alone at every instant when life affords us pause.

'And life is full of pauses which we can either seize on or waste.

'On the gloomiest, greyest days, what delight to think of all those intimate conversations yet to come!'

'What delight to know that we can raise our eyes to your face while the stew is thickening, while the telephone is giving the ringing-tone, while waiting at the bus-stop for the bus that never seems to come, while going upstairs, while going down the garden path to pick a sprig of parsley to put on the fish!'

What odd 'wildernesses' she reveals to us!

It is said that, one day, Jeanne de Chantal asked St. Francis of Sales whether he had said his prayers. 'No, daughter, not today,' but showing her a huge bundle of letters, he added, 'I have done something just as valuable.' We should beware of too glibly saying: I am doing my work, and hence I am praying. This happened towards the end of St. Francis's life. He had spent years in prayer and might justifiably think that answering his mail was the equivalent of praying. We should be cautious: we aren't St. Francis of Sales . . . yet . . .

Yesterday, today and tomorrow, ignorant or cultivated, monk, labourer or electrician: daily life in the presence of God is still the secret of prayer and of inner peace. Here we can quote Brother Lawrence of the Resurrection, a Carmelite lay-brother, whose entire life was lived in the presence of God. 'From my novitiate onwards,' he said, 'I strove to convince myself of the truth of this infinite Being' – i.e. that the

presence of God was not some vague idea – 'and hence, being
quite penetrated by the grandeur of this infinite Being, I shut
myself up in the place to which obedience had assigned me:
which was the kitchen.' Sometimes a host of wild thoughts
would force their way into his mind in place of God, but he
would gently push them aside. 'The time for action,' he would
say, 'is not different from that for prayer. I possess God as
tranquilly in the clatter of my kitchen, where sometimes
several people are asking for different things at once, as if I
were on my knees before the Blessed Sacrament.' But this
pre-supposes, of course, that we have already reached the
point of living in the presence of God. 'And,' he goes on, 'in
the way of God, thoughts do not matter much; love is what
counts.' God doesn't weigh the quantity of things that we have
done, but weighs the love with which we have done them:

'It is not necessary to have great things to do. In the kitchen,
I turn my little omelette in the frying pan for love of God;
when it is cooked, if I have nothing to do, I prostrate myself on
the floor and adore my God who has given me the grace to
cook it; after which I stand up, happier than a king. When I
cannot do anything else, it is enough for me if I pick a straw off
the ground for love of God.'

His superiors sent him from Paris to Burgundy, to fetch
some wine. Brother Lawrence had a withered leg; he was a
cripple. He could not move about in the boat, except by rolling himself along on the barrels, but he didn't worry about
that, because he knew that God was present. Great peace in
activity comes to us by use of humble means to the presence of
God.

'Walk in my presence and be perfect.' Why does walking in
God's presence lead to perfection? Because all day long, as
long as we live, this confronts us with Christ's saying, admit-
ting no exception: 'He who will not renounce all his
possessions, cannot be my disciple.' We have to 'stop being
anywhere, clinging to a place, a thing, a being, a hope,' as
Gustave Thibon remarks. This is not indifference but the high
freedom of love, truly loving – and more than ordinarily –
beings, things, words, world, but in the light of God, 'burning

yet not consuming,' like the flame of the Burning Bush.

We then become radio stations on the theological wavelength. Events, whatever come, being lived in faith and hope:

'My God, I believe ... I hope ... '

Why?

'Because you have said it ... because you have promised it ... because you are true ... because you are faithful' ...

Whatever happens, our support is in this 'because', *because God is God*.

What about charity?

'Because Jesus loved me and sacrificed himself for my sake' (*Ga* 2:20).

'*Because* God loved the world so much that he gave his only Son, so that anyone who believes in him will not be lost but will have eternal life' (*Jn* 3:16).